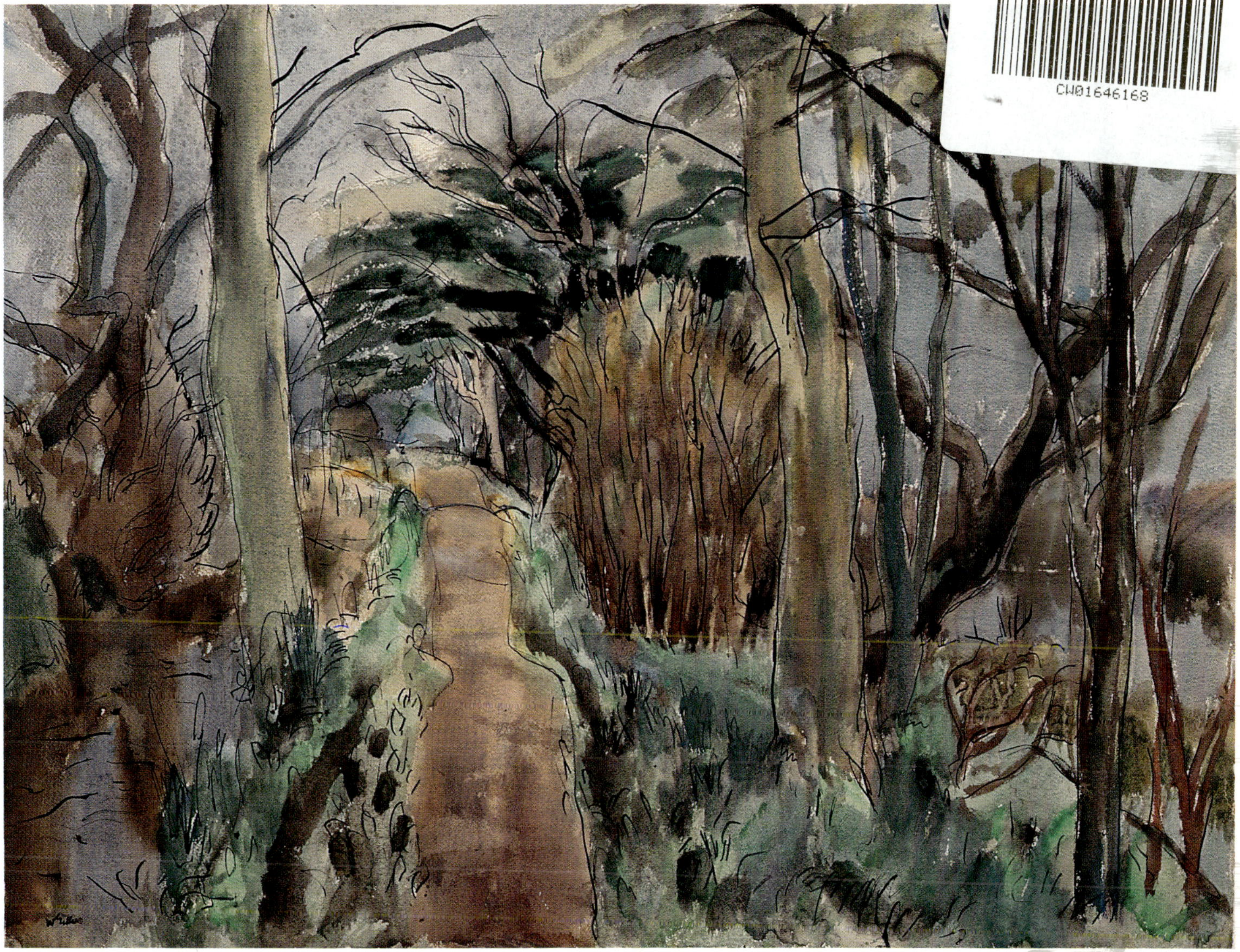

W. Gillies.

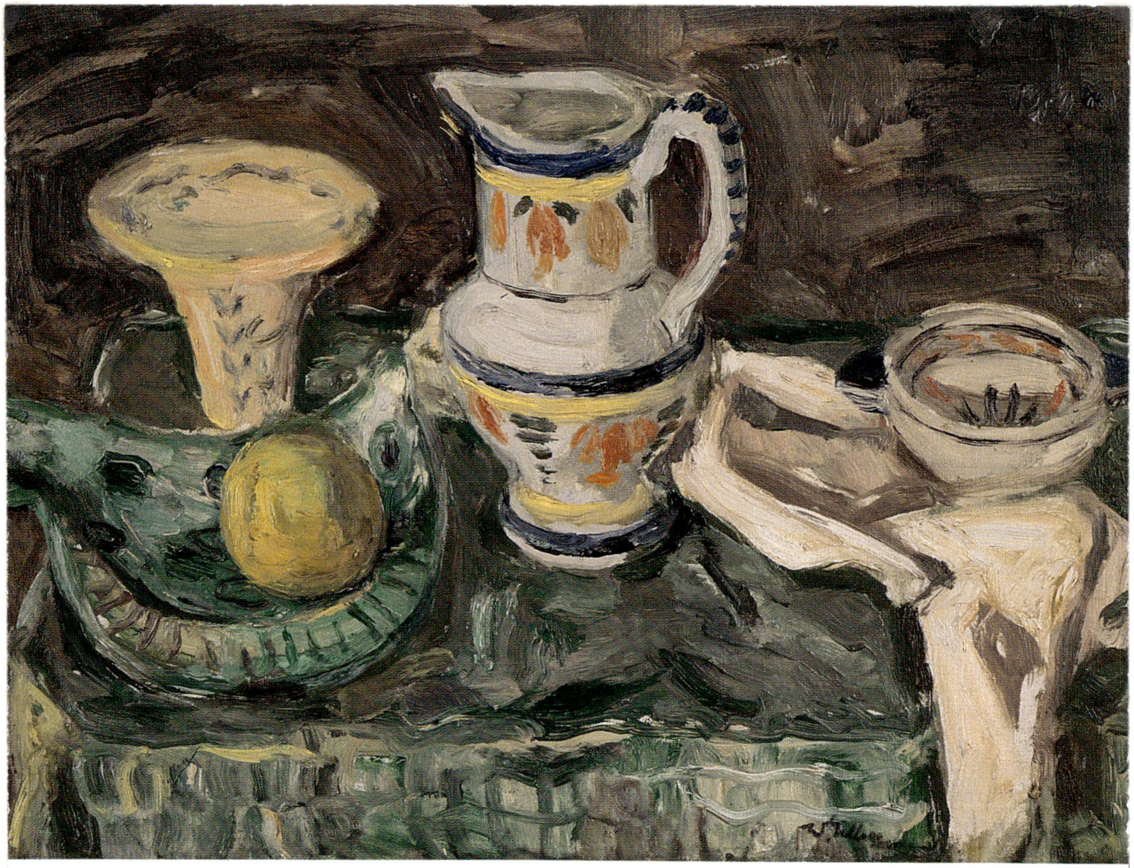

The Breton Pot

WILLIAM GILLIES · WATERCOLOURS OF SCOTLAND

SPONSORED BY

ATLAS HYDRAULIC LOADERS LTD
CRANES & EXCAVATORS

bsis
Matched

Atlas Hydraulic Loaders Ltd is an award winner under the
Business Sponsorship Incentive Scheme for its support of *William Gillies*.
The BSIS is a Government Scheme administered by the
Association for Business Sponsorship of the Arts.

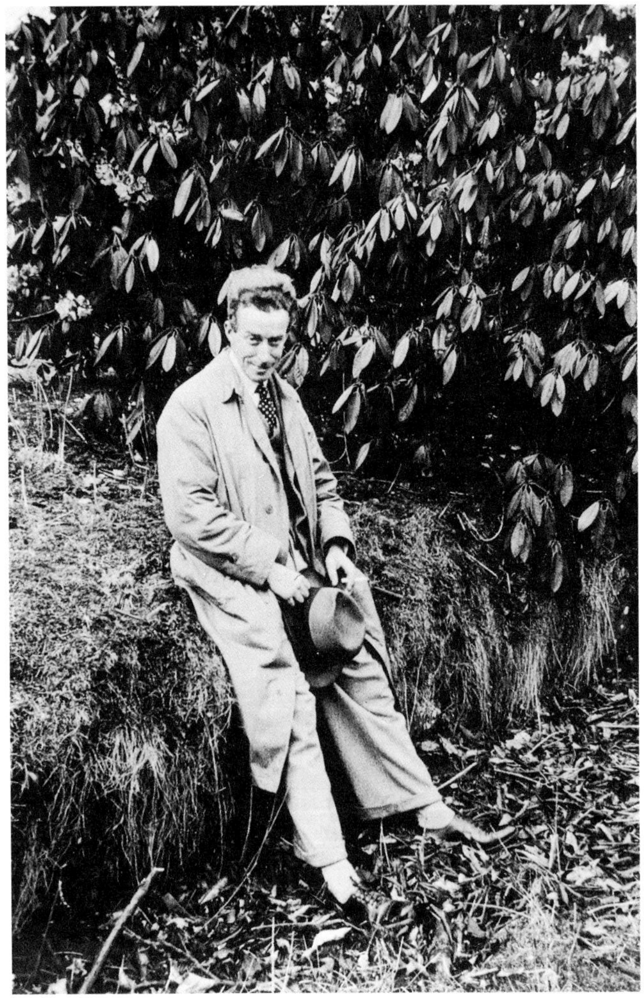

WILLIAM GILLIES

WATERCOLOURS OF SCOTLAND

BY PHILIP LONG

NATIONAL GALLERIES OF SCOTLAND
1994

Published by the Trustees
of the National Galleries of Scotland
for the exhibition *William Gillies · Watercolours of Scotland*
held at the Scottish National Gallery of Modern Art
Edinburgh, 7 July – 25 September 1994

ISBN 0 903598 48 5

Cover illustration:
Detail from *Wind above Kirriemuir*
catalogue 31

Photography by Antonia Reeve
Designed and typeset in Monotype Plantin by Dalrymple
Black and white photographs reproduced by kind permission of the Royal Scottish Academy
Maps reproduced by kind permission of Bartholomew's, a division of HarperCollins
Printed by Pale Green Press

Preface

The Scottish National Gallery of Modern Art owns 176 works by Sir William Gillies, the vast majority of which were bequeathed by Dr Robert Alexander Lillie. Born in Broughty Ferry, Lillie grew up in Aberdeen and then studied at Edinburgh University. From his youth he suffered ill-health and was unable to follow any formal career. This did not prevent him from fervently pursuing interests in music (his Edinburgh bungalow contained three pianos, two of them grands), philosophy, literature, and art. Lillie bought his first painting in 1940 and by the end of his life, in addition to works by, among others, Sickert, Boudin, and Pissarro, he had amassed one of the best collections of modern Scottish paintings.

In 1962 part of his collection was exhibited at the Scottish National Gallery of Modern Art, then recently opened at Inverleith House. The warm response this received confirmed Lillie's wish to bequeath the choice of his collection to the nation and, following his death in 1977, 299 works, selected from a total of over 600, passed to the permanent collections of the National Galleries of Scotland. It is due to Lillie's generosity, and to the bequest of Keith Andrews, former Keeper of Prints and Drawings at the National Gallery of Scotland, that it has not been necessary to borrow works for this exhibition, which so fully represents Gillies's achievements as a watercolourist.

In this catalogue, prepared and written by Philip Long, Research Assistant at the Gallery of Modern Art, we have reproduced Gillies's own photographs taken throughout his career and especially on his various painting expeditions around Scotland; with one exception, these are reproduced for the first time. Gillies also wrote numerous postcards to family and friends, and whenever possible his written comments have been related to specific works in the exhibition. We are most grateful to the Royal Scottish Academy for their permission to reproduce Gillies's photographs and for their kindness in lending a selection of both these and Gillies's postcards for display in the exhibition. We are indebted to Joanna Soden for her help in this. We would also like to thank Ken Winch of Bartholomew's for identifying appropriate maps of the period, reproduced here as endpapers.

Finally, we would like to thank Atlas Hydraulic Loaders Ltd for enthusiastically agreeing to sponsor the exhibition, for which they have qualified for a BSIS award. We hope it will be the start of a long and happy relationship.

TIMOTHY CLIFFORD
Director, National Galleries of Scotland

RICHARD CALVOCORESSI
Keeper, Scottish National Gallery of Modern Art

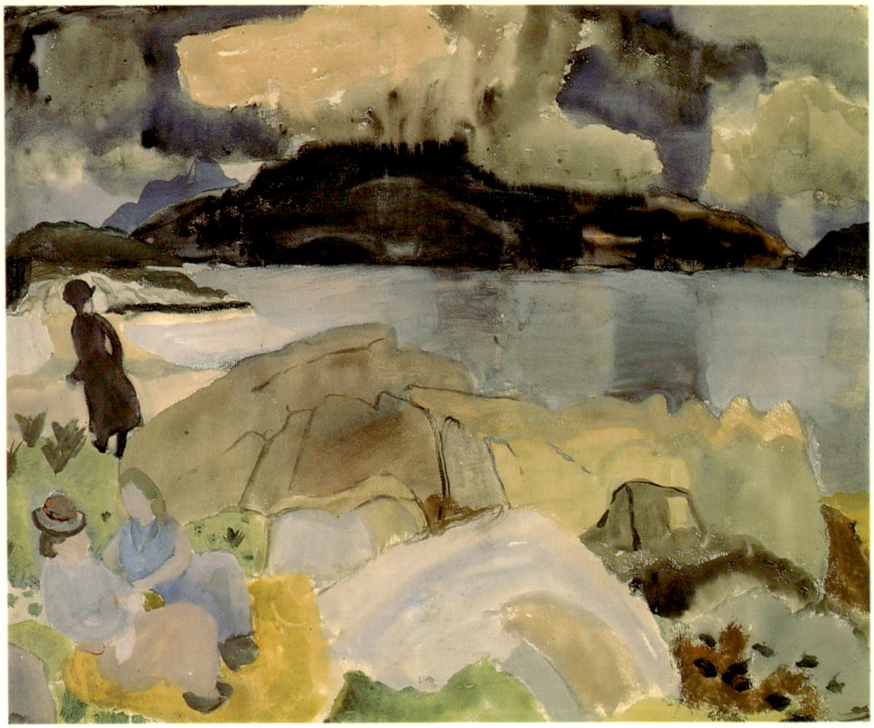

Introduction

WILLIAM GILLIES is recognised as one of the most important Scottish artists of the twentieth century. In a long and distinguished career he became Principal of his former college, Edinburgh College of Art, and received a succession of honours, culminating in a knighthood in recognition of services to the arts in Scotland. He had no particular desire for public attention and he is remembered by his students as a shy man; but great dedication and natural ability brought him, almost in spite of himself, to positions of considerable authority. As a young, gifted student he went to Paris in the mid-1920s and, like so many of his contemporaries, was influenced by the radical developments in art taking place there. In his more formal oil-paintings, which were for many the highlight of the annual exhibitions of the Royal Scottish Academy, his style would always remain freely eclectic and he openly admitted to the influence of Bonnard, Vuillard, Matisse and, latterly, Braque on his work and particularly on his still lifes. In his landscapes in watercolour, however, painted directly from nature, he responded freely and intuitively to his subject-matter, producing works of beauty, insight and originality.

William George Gillies was born in Haddington, East Lothian, on 21 September, 1898. His father, John Gillies, was the proprietor of a tobacconist in Haddington's High Street and William's early childhood was spent in a house above the shop. Later, as their circumstances improved, the Gillies family, John, his wife Emma, and their three children Janet, William and Emma, moved to a newly-built house, Westlea, at Meadow Park on the edge of the town.

Gillies attended Haddington's local preparatory school and then the Knox Institute (now the Knox Academy) where his aptitude for drawing and painting was actively encouraged. There were no specialist art teachers at the Knox Institute and Gillies's developing enthusiasm for art was more the result of several personal associations: the most important of these was William Ryle Smith, his uncle. Art Master at the Grove Academy, Broughty Ferry, Ryle Smith regularly visited his sister and her family in Haddington during the summer holidays. The young Gillies accompanied him on sketching and painting expeditions into the picturesque closes of Haddington and the neighbouring countryside. More significantly, Ryle Smith introduced him to *The Studio*, the leading British journal devoted to contemporary international fine and applied art: its richly illustrated pages carried reviews of exhibitions from across the European continent. Ryle Smith also took him to the annual exhibitions of the Royal Scottish Academy, the Society of Scottish Artists and the Royal Glasgow Institute and to the permanent collections of the National Gallery of Scotland and Dundee City Art Gallery. In Broughty Ferry, there was the opportunity to examine Ryle Smith's own small collection of mostly Scottish paintings. Thomas Elder Dickson, Gillies's biographer, recalls that Gillies was particularly impressed by two works by the highly gifted but then little-known Forfar-born painter James Watterston Herald (1859–1914) whose sensitive, restrained, deeply atmospheric watercolour style had been influenced by the 'blottesque' technique of Arthur Melville (1855–1904).[1] *A Corner of Kirrie* [i.e. Kirriemuir, figure 1], painted by Gillies at around the age of fourteen and signed additionally by his uncle, demonstrates this early influence but he arrived at a bolder, more stylised expression in his smaller ink drawings and watercolours [figure 2], which emulate the graphic technique of artists such as Allen W. Seaby and the Edinburgh-born Thomas Austen Brown, whose work featured regularly in journals like *The Studio*.

Further opportunity to study examples of recent painting came from Gillies's early friendship with a local Haddington figure, Robert Alexander Dakers, editor of *The Haddington Courier*, and a collector of Scottish art. Since the late nineteenth century the gentle, rolling countryside of East Lothian, bounded to the south by the Lammermuir Hills and to the north by the coast of the Firth of Forth, had been popular with Scottish artists who, influenced by the romantic realism of the French Barbizon painters and by the Dutch Hague School, favoured idyllic, pastoral, subject matter. In 1883 James Guthrie (1859–1930) and others of the Glasgow School had established Cockburnspath on the east coast as a popular artists' colony and by the early twentieth century something of an East Coast School had been formed around painters such as James Campbell Noble (1846–1913), his cousin Robert Noble (1857–1917) and William Darling McKay (1844–1924), who lived or had spent extended periods

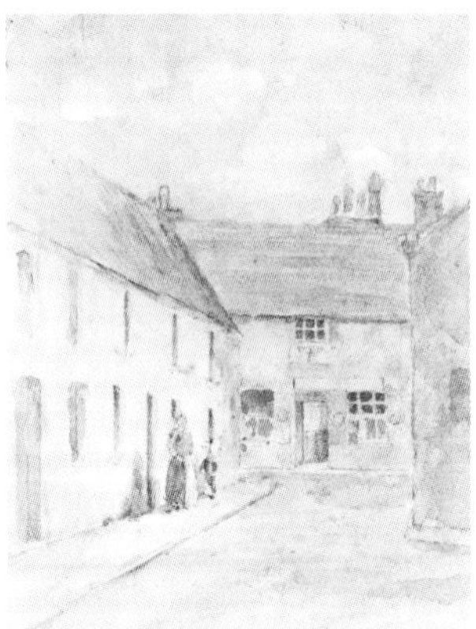

figure 1 *A Corner of Kirrie* dated 1912
watercolour and pencil on paper, 23 × 18cm
Royal Scottish Academy

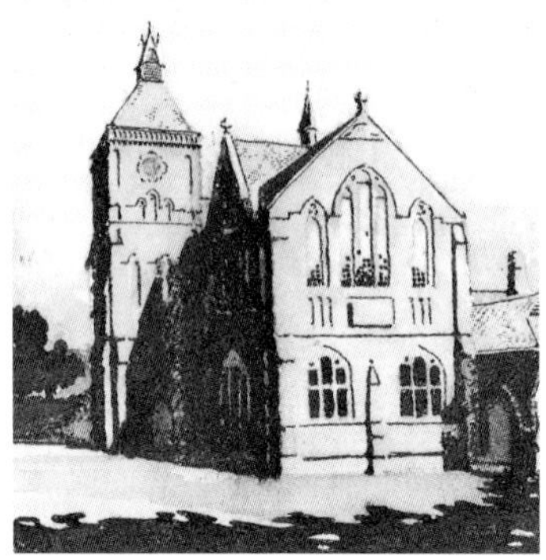

figure 2 *Study of a Church circa* 1914
watercolour and ink on paper, 12 × 10.7cm
Royal Scottish Academy

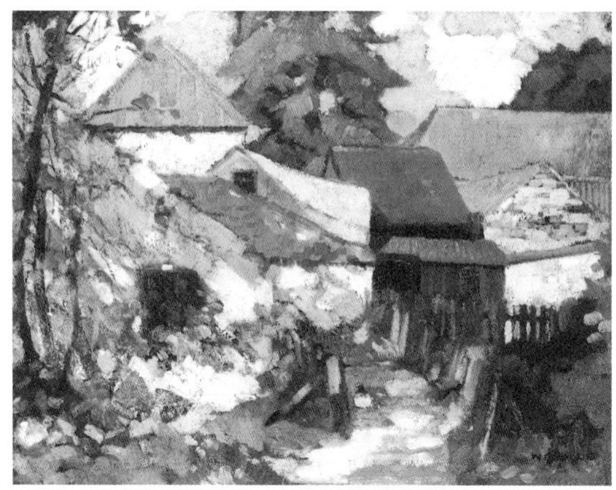

figure 3 *Sunshine, Cramond circa* 1916–21
oil on canvas, 35.7 × 46
Scottish National Gallery of Modern Art

working in the countryside around the rural villages of Haddington, Gifford and East Linton. It was art of this type that Dakers admired and collected and which he emulated in his own paintings which were regularly hung at the Royal Scottish Academy. Gillies joined Dakers on painting expeditions and by his late teens had evolved a corresponding style, painting rural landscape compositions, such as *Sunshine, Cramond* [figure 3], in broadly applied oil, frequently enlivened by picturesque lighting effects.

In 1916 Gillies left the Knox Institute with the Dux Medal, awarded to the best pupil of the year, and in the autumn began his studies at Edinburgh College of Art. In April 1917 he received his call-up papers. Drafted to France with the Scottish Rifles he saw service in the trenches around Arras. Wounded and gassed on the western front in 1918, he was sent back to Scotland to recuperate and was finally discharged from the army in the spring of 1919. Recalling these dark times more than half a century later he described his war experience as 'Two wasted years … when I'm asked my age I always subtract these two'.[2]

He returned to the College in October 1919, passing directly into the second year of the general preliminary course which all students were required to complete before beginning their chosen Diploma Course. Edinburgh College of Art had been established in 1908 by the city council to serve as a central institution for art education in Edinburgh and south-east Scotland. Despite this enlightened attempt to coordinate and improve upon the standard of art education available in the east, the College's syllabus remained firmly academic, inheriting the nineteenth-century discipline of one of the institutions it replaced, Edinburgh's first publicly-founded art school, the Trustees' Academy. Students undertaking the Diploma course in the School of Drawing and Painting were routinely expected, under the direction of the Head of the Department David Alison (1882–1955), to complete courses in drawing and painting (from life, draped life and from the antique), studies in anatomy, exercises in composition, and studies in art history.[3] The didactic character of the teaching method is indicated by titles of two of the topics included in the syllabus: 'Study and Demonstration of the General Technical Process in the Evolution of a Picture' and 'Study of the Principles of Pictorial Composition and their application as shown in the work of the Masters'.[4] The formality of the College's teaching, with its emphasis on draughtsmanship and on technical ability, did, however, provide a foundation for the development of some of the most enduring and influential Scottish artistic talents of this century. In the years Gillies attended the College his fellow students included William Crozier (1897–1930), William MacTaggart (1903–1981), grandson of the great nineteenth-century landscape painter,

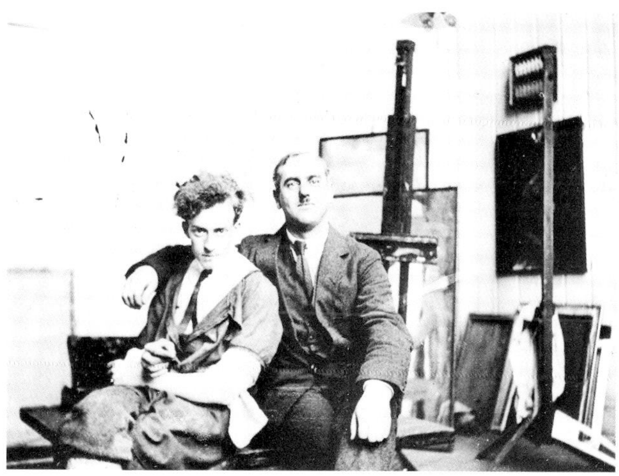

Gillies as a student at Edinburgh College of Art, with unidentified tutor, 1923

John Maxwell (1905–1962), Anne Redpath (1895–1965), and William Johnstone (1897–1981). Johnstone, whose work in the 1930s was amongst the most radical being produced in Britain, moved away from Scotland in 1931, but the example set in particular by MacTaggart, Maxwell and Gillies, both in their dedication to painting and in their long careers as teachers at Edinburgh College of Art, would influence several generations of Scottish artists. Gillies's conscientious student work was rewarded in 1921 when he was granted a small bursary enabling him to travel to London where he visited the National and Tate Galleries.[5] In 1922 he received his Diploma, highly commended, and was awarded a post-Diploma scholarship which gave him studio facilities at the College for a further year.

For the many Scottish art students who graduated in the years immediately after the First World War there were few opportunites to exhibit. In 1891 the Society of Scottish Artists had been established, partly in reaction to the conservatism of the Royal Scottish Academy, with the worthy aim of 'holding an Annual Exhibition in Edinburgh, to give inducement to the younger Artists to produce more important and original works by providing hanging space for such works'.[6] More modest in scale were the succession of professional exhibiting societies created in the early years of this century such as the Edinburgh Group, founded in 1912; the Society of Eight, also founded in 1912; and the Glasgow Society of Painters and Sculptors, founded in 1919, each of which was made up of an exclusive membership. During Gillies's scholarship year at the College he joined with a group of recent graduate students, and together they founded their own exhibiting society, the 1922 Group, the name derived from the year in which most had obtained their Diplomas. For Gillies and the other members their annual exhibitions, held from 1923 to 1929 at the New Gallery in Edinburgh's Shandwick Place, would have provided them with their first opportunity to exhibit work as professional artists.[7]

Following Gillies's completion of his post-Diploma studies he was recommended for a travelling scholarship 'awarded each year to a student of exceptional ability'.[8] Exceptionally that year, the College awarded an additional scholarship, to Gillies's contemporary William Geissler (1896–1963). On the recommendation of the College Principal, Frank Morley Fletcher (1866–1949), they went to Paris, enrolling at the Académie Montparnasse, the academy of art opened by André Lhote (1885–1962) in 1922. By the early years of the twentieth century France had become a natural choice for ambitious young Scottish painters wishing to continue their education abroad. French realist painting had crucially influenced the development of the Glasgow School and several of the Glasgow Boys, namely John Lavery, William Kennedy, Alexander Roche and Thomas Millie Dow, had gone to France in the early 1880s to study in the Paris ateliers and to work *en plein air* in the artists' colonies around Fontainebleau. Their example was, in turn, to influence four of the most important artists of the succeeding generation, Samuel John Peploe (1871–1935), George Leslie Hunter (1879–1931), Francis Campbell Boileau Cadell (1883–1937) and John Duncan Fergusson (1874–1961), all of whom spent extended periods living and working in France. Peploe, Hunter, Cadell and Fergusson, later to become collectively known as the Scottish Colourists, were among the first British painters to make direct contact with French Post-Impressionist painting, and for Gillies and his contemporaries graduating from the Scottish art colleges in the 1920s they represented a direct link with artists like Gauguin, Derain, Matisse and van Gogh, whose work they would have encountered in contemporary art magazines.

Fergusson in particular had formed close associations

with many of the leading figures of the avant-garde in Paris and to the younger generation of aspiring Scottish artists must have seemed an impressive figure. Moreover, at the time of Gillies's graduation, all four of the Colourists were at the height of their commercial success, exhibiting and regularly selling their work at the Royal Scottish Academy and through the dealers Aitken Dott (The Scottish Gallery) in Edinburgh, and Alexander Reid in Glasgow.

For Gillies, travelling to Paris to study under André Lhote must have presented an exciting prospect. Lhote's close and early association with the Cubist movement would have made him a logical choice as a teacher to young and aspiring artists wishing to learn about the very latest developments in painting. The spirit of invention which so enriched the work of the protagonists of the Cubist movement did not, however, extend to Lhote's own painting or to his teaching methods. Gillies recalled:

What started off as appearing to be a new and exciting way of producing pictures in the end turned out to be a dismal cul-de-sac. I did not long employ Lhote's principles in my painting ... The hours were long and constant, so that we came into contact with no other French painters ... We went to exhibitions or out sketching at the weekends ... that was all.[9]

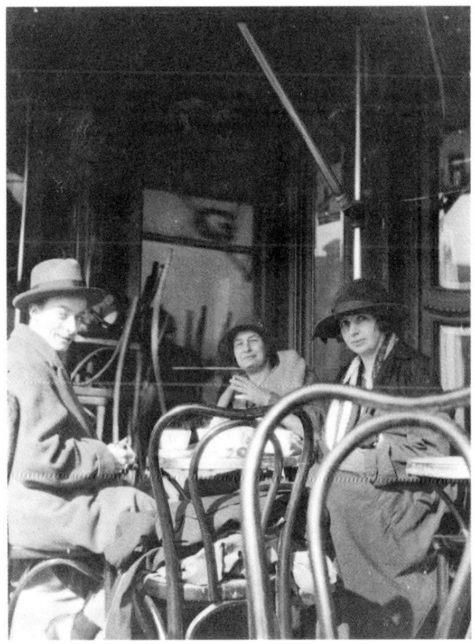

Gillies in Paris 1923–24

In spite of these later criticisms, Lhote's programmatic approach to picture-making certainly made an impact, however short-lived, on Gillies and on other Scots, in particular William Crozier, who also studied with Lhote in Paris in the 1920s. And if Lhote's methods did not provide the liberating experience Gillies might have hoped for after completing five years of disciplined, methodical study in Edinburgh, he was, nevertheless, able to see in Paris work by artists such as André Derain and the more 'natural' and 'expressive' painting of Maurice de Vlaminck, Chaïm Soutine and André Dunoyer de Segonzac which would affect the development of his own style.

Shortly after Gillies's return to Scotland in 1924 he was appointed to his first professional post, as Assistant Art Master at the Royal Academy in Inverness. Few examples of his work are known from this period in his career. One watercolour, labelled and dated 'Inverness 1925' [figure 4], was bequeathed with the remainder of his estate to the Royal Scottish Academy upon his death in 1973; however, nothing about the composition itself connects it with any particular aspect of the Scottish landscape. Gillies is attracted by the abstract qualities of the view ahead of him, by the triangular forms of the cottage roofs and gables repeated in the rigging of the ship at anchor, utilising these as elements in the overall design. This formalising approach to picture-making is clearly indebted to the methods he would have learned from Lhote.

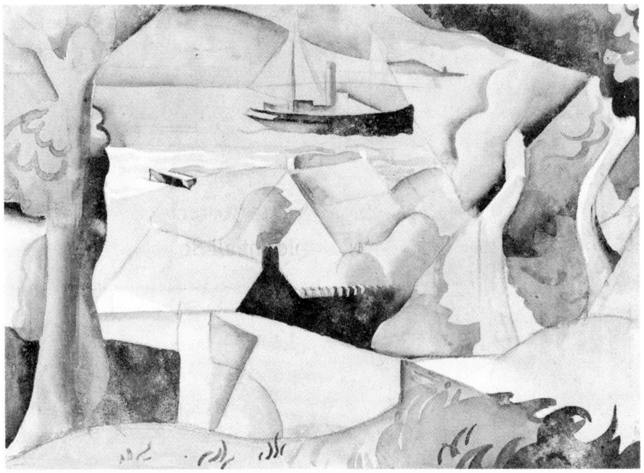

figure 4 *Inverness* 1925
watercolour and pencil on paper, 25.4 × 35.4 cm
Royal Scottish Academy

In 1925, a year after taking up his appointment at Inverness, he received an invitation to return to Edinburgh College of Art, this time to a part-time teaching post as an assistant to his old Head of School David Alison. Geissler too was appointed but was to leave in 1927 to become art master at Perth Academy.[10] For Gillies, however, it was the beginning of a teaching career at the College that would last for forty years.

Gillies quickly became a central figure in the artistic community of Edinburgh. Former lecturers such as David MacBeth Sutherland (1883–1973), Adam Bruce Thomson (1885–1976) and Donald Moodie (1892–1963) now became his colleagues and friends. In 1928 he moved with his family to Willlowbrae Road in Edinburgh and, following the premature death of William Crozier, took up the latter's old studio space at 45 Frederick Street, which was shared with MacTaggart. The progressive work Gillies exhibited at this time at the annual exhibitions of the 1922 Group earned him a reputation as something of an artistic rebel, and he later recalled an Edinburgh professor from this early period in his career 'buying a picture of mine, "fast, before I went completely mad"'.[11]

Gillies's sister Janet was to recall later in her life:

When I look back to our childhood days I feel so thankful we were all born in Haddington and the grand East Lothian farms all around us. We spent our young days rambling among the farms and country lanes. He [Gillies] *used to sketch so well and got such enjoyment out of life.*[12]

Working in and enjoying the open air was to become an integral part of Gillies's life and he would spend his time occupied in this way whenever he was able. From his days as a student at Edinburgh, weekends would be spent with like-minded companions on painting trips into the surrounding countryside and during the long college vacations these sorties became more ambitious with camping expeditions to remote parts of the Highlands, to Perthshire, the countryside around the Solway Firth, and to the fishing villages of Fife. Asked how he spent one past holiday he replied 'Why painting, of course, what else is there to do?'.[13]

His most regular companion on these expeditions was John Maxwell, whose studies at Edinburgh College of Art, from 1921–26, had overlapped with Gillies's own. Maxwell was from Dalbeattie, in Kircudbrightshire, and Gillies accompanied him there on the first painting trip they made together in 1929, the year in which Maxwell was appointed to the College staff. In *Morning Light, Kircudbright Farm* [figure 5], likely to have been painted on this expedition, Gillies has again been drawn to the naturally abstract forms in the landscape, structuring his design around the road and the solid masses of farm buildings boldly silhouettted in harsh sunlight against a backdrop of empty sky. *Near Kircudbright* [figure 6] is a more traditionally composed view of the gentle countryside around the Solway Firth, the perspectival device of sharply tapering country road emphasizing the spatial depth of the composition.

In contrast to the emotional, expressive, painterly style Gillies was to develop in the 1930s, his approach to landscape painting in the mid- to late-1920s can in retrospect be characterised by a self-conscious formality, indebted in part to Lhote's teaching and to the ideology of continental modernism. These qualities in his work, combined with his natural ability as a draughtsman, helped establish his reputation as one of the most interesting young artists working in Scotland. In 1932 his talent was formally recognised by his election to the exclusive Society of Eight, whose distinguished members were David Alison, F. C. B. Cadell, John Duncan, Sir John Lavery, Henry Lintott, James Paterson and S. J. Peploe, then amongst the most senior figures in the Scottish art world.

In addition to providing exhibiting opportunities for the more progressive types of art being produced in Scotland, the Society of Scottish Artists aimed to foster this process by bringing to its exhibitions 'examples of all Schools of Modern Art from distinguished living Artists, foreign as well as native'.[14] In previous years, for example, the organisers had secured works by Monet, Rousseau, Cézanne, Gauguin, Matisse, van Gogh, Severini and Picasso to show alongside submitted entries at its annual exhibitions. In 1931 twelve works by the Norwegian artist Edvard Munch (1863–1944) were shown by the Society.[15] Munch's art was then little-

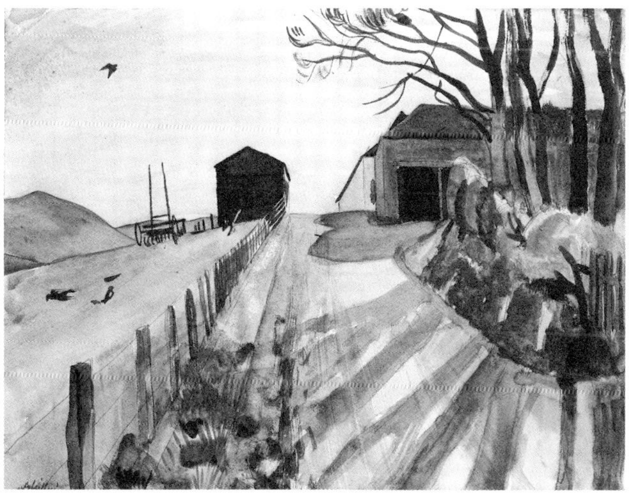

figure 5 *Morning Light, Kircudbright Farm* *circa* 1929
catalogue 2

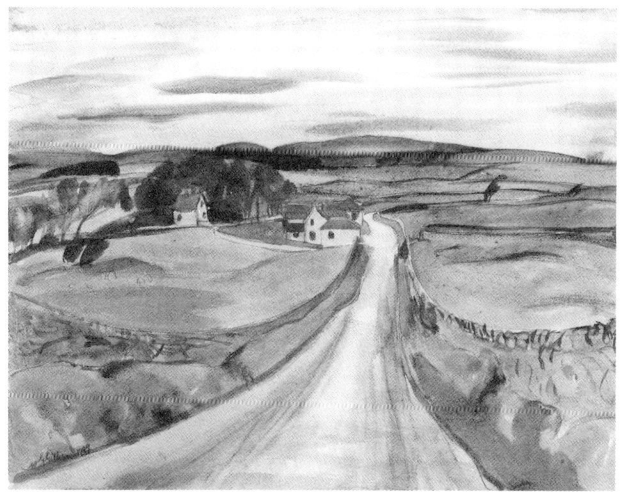

figure 6 *Near Kirkudbright* dated 1929
catalogue 3

known in Britain and whilst the exhibition of his work in Edinburgh was not to cause the controversy it had on previous occasions elsewhere, it did provide a focus for a wider cultural debate, centred around the 'Scottish Renaissance' movement.[16] This concerned whether there was, or indeed whether there ought to be, a particular native cultural identity, or authentic 'School' of art, conditioned by the native temperament, which might be distinctive to Scotland as a nation. It was argued, for example, by amongst others Herbert Read, then Professor of Fine Art at Edinburgh University, that the expressive, vigorously painted works by Munch had a distinctive Nordic sensibilty, a sensibilty which could be particularly appreciated by the exhibition's northern European audience and which might therefore be a more appropriate model for Scottish artists who had for some time looked customarily to France for artistic direction. Munch's work certainly affected Gillies. Elder Dickson recalled that it 'shook' him and added:[17]

Although not unaware of the existence of the Expressionist movement, he was quite unprepared for this startling confrontation. Fascinated, mystified, his critical faculties paralysed, he returned to the exhibition time and time again to take in as much as he could assimilate. Everything now seemed tame and spineless compared with this 'naked thinking heart'.[18]

Gillies's landscapes from the early 1930s contain an emotional response to his subject matter that is not present in the earlier work. The refined pencil lines and cautious handling of watercolour in his Kircudbrightshire landscapes from 1929 are replaced in *A Pool* [plate 3] by broad chalk, describing with an impetuous energy the dark mass of surrounding trees; and in *The Dark Pond* [plate 6] deep, vibrant watercolour is thickly applied in a technique appropriate to the handling of oil paint. Munch's art cannot be considered independently from his private life, which was marked by personal tragedy and by deep mental neurosis. Gillies too suffered close personal loss (his father and his younger sister Emma were both to die prematurely), but he was of an essentially calm temperament and his adoption of an expressive technique was not motivated by any cathartic need. The inspiration in his work did not derive from a troubled psyche but from the endless variety he found in his subject-matter and in particular in landscape which was for him an unequalled source of joy and inspiration:

I have always enjoyed weather; always seen landscape pictorially, and I've got immense satisfaction in recording in line and colour the fugitive, the subtle and the grand in nature.[19]

To Gillies and his contemporaries, Munch's painting must have represented, most powerfully, a radical alternative to a formalised method of picture-making.

Throughout the 1930s Gillies continued his trips around Scotland, sketching and painting in the company of friends. He had a passion for motor cars and owned a succession of large, fast vehicles in which he was able to ferry his companions, their painting materials and their tents. His most regular destination at this time was the Highlands and in particular the west coast where the tremendously powerful country around Ardnamurchan, Morar and the Kyle of Lochalsh, was to provide inspiration for some of his most poetic interpretations of landscape. Watercolour was an ideal, portable medium for painting on these expeditions, and it is tempting to draw a comparison between its fluid, transparent nature and the characteristically vaporous Scottish atmosphere. In watercolour Gillies was able to respond quickly, recording in broad strokes of a hog's-hair brush the shifting light and weather conditions of the mountainous coast. *Skye Hills from near Morar* [plate 4], painted in *circa* 1931, is one of Gillies's finest works from this period. Passages of luminescent watercolour lyrically describe the steep

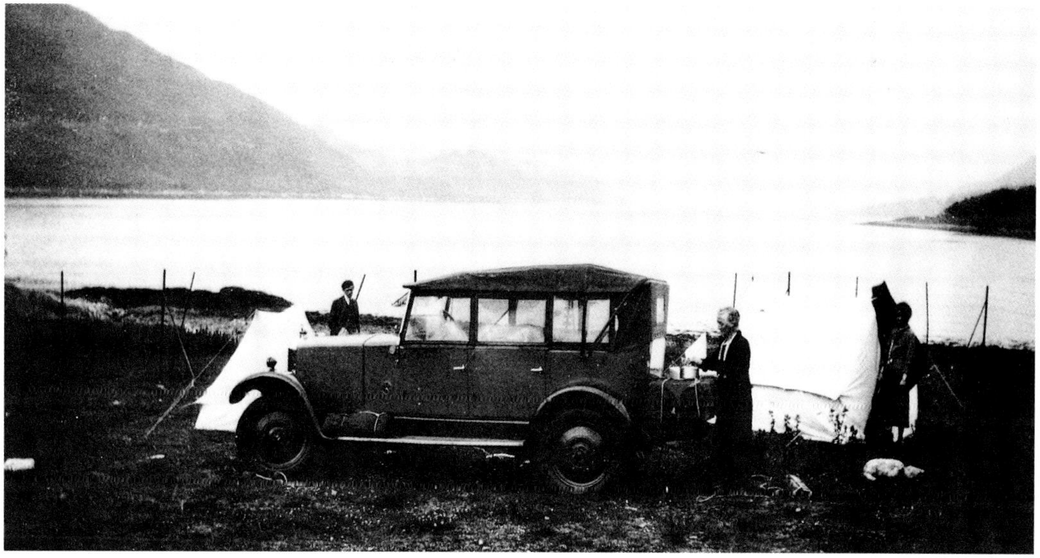

Setting up Camp *left to right* unknown, Gillies's mother, his sister Jenny

banks of cloud rolling towards the viewer from the wide horizon, which is punctuated by the mystical profile of the Cuillin Hills.

Gillies's prodigious output on these expeditions could prove frustrating to his companions, not least to Maxwell whose approach to painting was far more deliberate. The artist David McClure, who studied under both, described how 'Gillies would complete half-a-dozen watercolours before lunch, while Maxwell would still be contemplating some suitable aspect of his subject'.[20] Gillies's postcards home to his sisters indicate, however, the careless existence and simple pleasures of these painting holidays, concerned with little more than a fine spot for that night's camping or a hospitable farmhouse that would provide an evening meal. He later summed up these expeditions with the words 'We worked hard, we enjoyed ourseleves enormously and we covered most of Scotland this way'.[21] As his style evolved other influences would shape the development of his painting. The simplistic depiction of buildings and trees in *The Street* [plate 8], of *circa* 1933, connects Gillies's work with contemporary English painters such as Christopher Wood and Ben and Winifred Nicholson, who were then producing landscapes in a deliberately 'naïve' and simplified style. The extraordinarily expressive, child-like colouring in this composition, however, suggests an even closer relationship to the painting of Paul Klee whose work was exhibited at the Society of Scottish Artists in 1934.

In 1935 the regular order of Gillies's life was disrupted by the death after a period of illness of his younger sister Emma. Gillies had been particularly close to Emma and had painted several sensitive portraits of her. She had shared his artistic ambition, studying pottery at Edinburgh College of Art. *In Ardnamurchan* [plate 5], painted on a family holiday shortly after Emma's death, and incorporating the figures of his mother, his Aunt Margaret (in black fur coat and feathered hat) and his sister Jenny, is one of Gillies's finest watercolours and also one of his most unusual. Figures rarely appear in Gillies's landscapes and while they add a considerable and poignant charm to this composition, they appear as an integrated and minor part of Gillies's evocation of the grand natural scene before him. The figures have been identified from Gillies's own snapshot, which also confirms the work's topographical accuracy. It is most unlikely, however, that Gillies ever painted from photographs. The inherent vitality of his landscape painting can only be explained as the consequence of his experience of working directly from nature.

Gillies became a full-time member of staff at Edinburgh

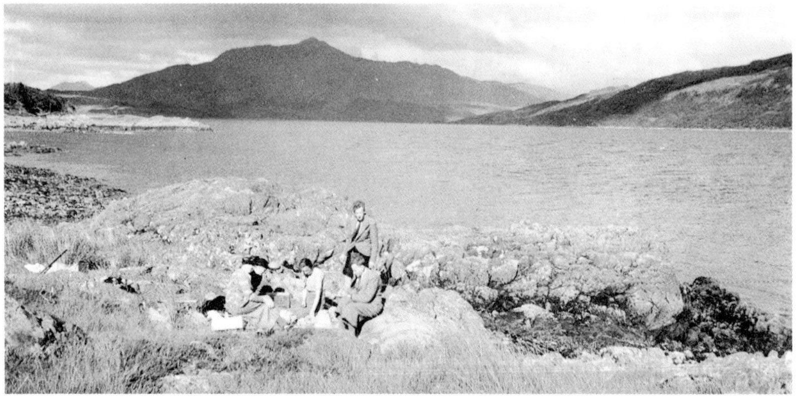

left to right The artists's mother, Aunt Margaret, sister Jenny, Gillies (standing) and an unidentified figure (seated), in Ardnamurchan (*cf.* plate 5), *circa* 1936

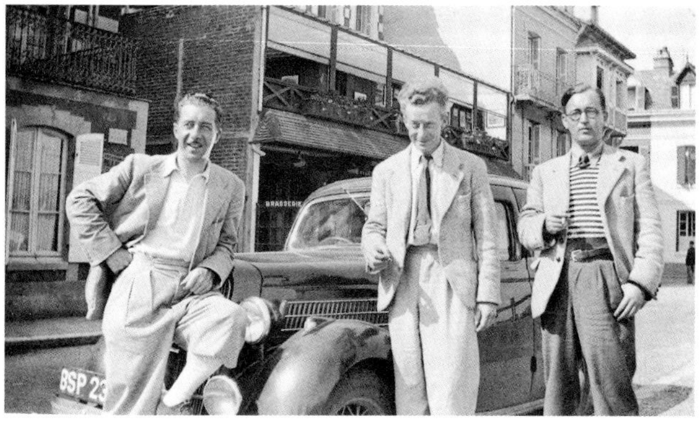

left to right Bill Logan, Gillies and John Maxwell in St-Valery, 1938

College of Art in 1934 and during term was left with only evenings and weekends to devote to his work. In the holidays the pattern of painting expeditions around Scotland continued. A rare visit abroad, to St-Valery on the north coast of France in 1938 in the company of Bill Logan and John Maxwell, resulted in some fine watercolours but, with the exception of particular topographical details, there is little to distinguish them from the many gaily-coloured works he would later make in the fishing villages of the East Neuk of Fife. In *Crofts, Bonar Bridge* [plate 10], dating from a visit to the area around the Dornoch Firth made in about 1938, Gillies first maps out the intricacies of the landscape in pen and ink before applying multi-coloured washes of paint. In his depictions of the west coast, Gillies had found little use for precisely defined line, but here the complex patterning of the crofters' farmland rising before him demanded a more constrained technique. The linear approach adopted in *Crofts, Bonar Bridge* demonstrates Gillies's sensitivity to landscape and the flexibilty of his artistic language to attune with each new choice of subject. It also indicates the later landscape style he was to develop.

In 1939 the Gillies family moved from Willowbrae Road to the village of Temple in Midlothian, approximately ten miles to the south of Edinburgh. This was to prove an ideal location and they were to spend the remainder of their lives there. Surrounded by farmland, Temple offered a return to peaceful rural life for William, his mother and sister, while remaining within easy commuting distance of Edinburgh. Significantly, too, it was within easy reach of the Border countryside. Equipping himself with an Ariel motor cycle Gillies was able to explore in detail the expansive area covered by the Moorfoot and Lammermuir Hills stretching away south and east to the Border towns of Innerleithen, Galashiels, Melrose, and Kelso. The picturesque village of Temple itself and its immediate surroundings became a favourite area for painting, particularly when bad weather prevented him from working outside for any long period. In *Winter, Temple (Back of Houses)* [plate 15] he takes as his subject the complicated tangle of exposed trees and hedgerow, and draws it assertively in pen, against the snow-covered gardens, pantile-roofed cottages and harsh, grey-blue sky.

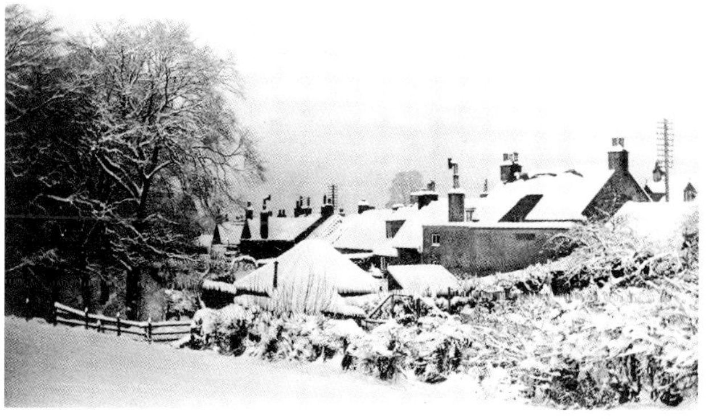

Temple, back of houses (*cf.* plate 15)

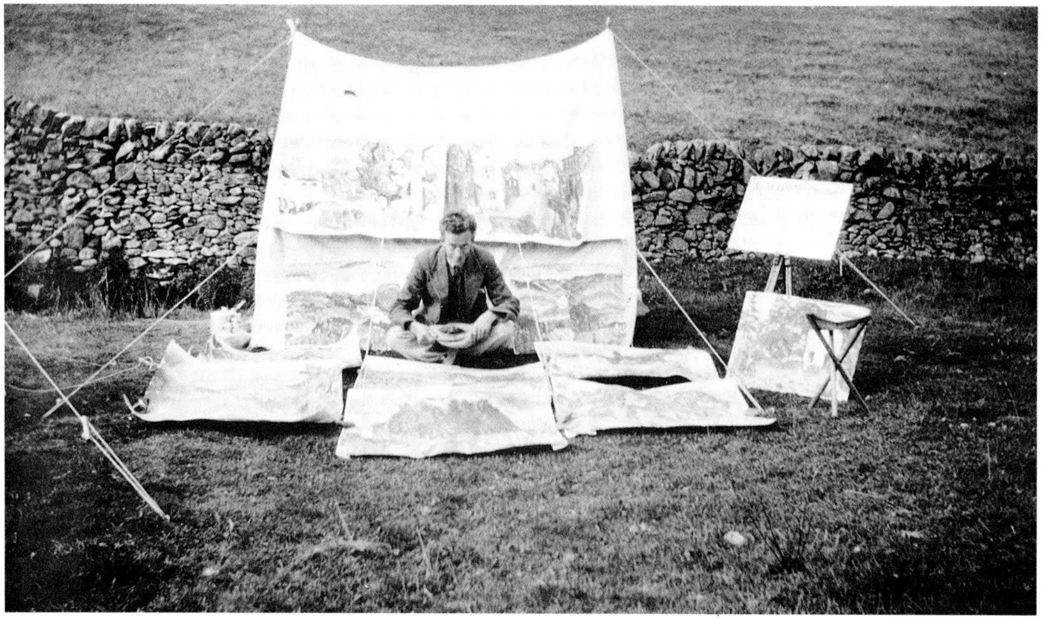

An impromptu exhibition of the artist's work: the placard on the easel reads 'The Calidon Show … Spare a Dime'

The most pronounced change in Gillies's treatment of landscape, dating from the 1940s and coinciding with his move to Temple, is the introduction of line, either in pen and ink or in softer pencil depending on the natural requirements of his subject-matter. With this he was able to give structure to the essential character of the Border landscape of farm and moorland and undulating hills, divided by winding roads and rivers, drystone dykes and railway lines. Although his use of line lends an air of restraint to works from this later period, *The Pond* for example [plate 13], in comparison to the bold, expressive handling of similar subjects from the early 1930s, Gillies always remained flexible in his approach. An extraordinary contrast to *Winter, Temple* is another back view of the village, *Landscape with Houses, Temple* [plate 14], where attempt to define form is set aside in the sheer lyrical enjoyment of describing the colour and heat of a summer's day.

During the war Gillies's travels were restricted but the pattern of painting expeditions began again soon afterwards. The fishing villages of east Fife became a favourite destination with repeated visits made from the late 1940s and through the 1950s to Pittenweem, Anstruther and St Monance. Whilst there he and his companions would often camp in the grounds of Kellie Castle, home of the sculptor Hew Lorimer (1907–93) who had studied at Edinburgh College of Art in the early 1930s. In views like *St Monance from the Harbour* [plate 16], Gillies, fascinated by the complex paraphernalia of the fisherman's profession, was able to exercise his skills as a draughtsman to the utmost, giving structure and volume to the string of lobster creels drying on the harbour wall. Postcards sent home from these holidays reveal his preferences for 'ideal' painting conditions. 'Getting really glorious weather – not very paintable, though sea too blue',[22] and again, 'Weather has been almost too good – for painting – no clouds at all – so output not as big as I'd like'.[23]

In 1946 Gillies was made Head of the the School of Drawing and Painting at Edinburgh College of Art, succeeding his old teacher David Alison. One of the first appointments he made to the staff was Robert Henderson Blyth (1919–1970), a recent graduate from Glasgow School of Art. With Blyth he visited the north coast of Moray in 1950 and 1951, drawing and painting the isolated fishing villages of Gardenstown [plate 19] and Crovie, located at the base of imposing red sandstone cliffs. In 1955 Gillies persuaded Maxwell to rejoin the College staff (he had 'retired' in 1943 to concentrate on his own work) and in the following year he returned to paint in the area around Maxwell's home, writing from the village of Kippford [plate 23], 'Have gone all round but found nothing as good as the country between Dalbeattie and the sea'.[24] Fishing villages continued to be a favourite destination. Later in 1956 he visited Eyemouth on the Berwickshire coast, this time in the company of John Houston (born 1930), a former student of the College and from 1954 a member of its staff.

Gillies's increasing teaching responsibilties inevitably encroached on the time he might otherwise have devoted to his own work. This was never to interfere, however, with his enjoyment of College life.

Far from being a burden…my teaching career has been a real delight to me … I feel that my contact with the attitudes of so many young and enthusiastic and idealistic students has prevented me from becoming the old fossil you might have expected me to grow into … Teaching in a college of art like Edinburgh is an inspiration.[25]

In spite of Gillies's teaching commitments he was always to remain an immensely prolific artist. In the 1930s he exhibited annually with the Society of Eight and throughout his career showed regularly with the Society of Scottish Artists, the Royal Scottish Society of Painters in Watercolour, of which he was made President, and the Royal Scottish

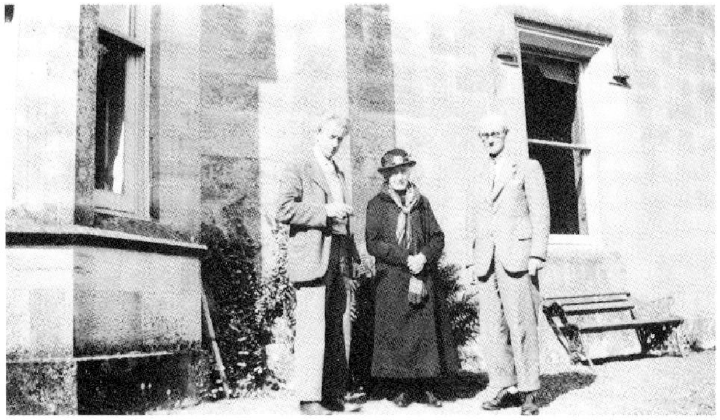

Gillies, his mother and Dr Lillie

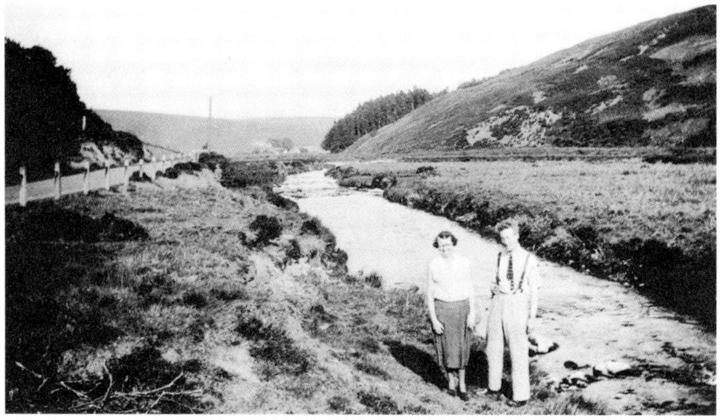

Gillies and his sister Jenny in the Lammermuir Hills

Academy. In 1940 the philosopher, musician and collector Dr Robert Alexander Lillie bought his first picture by Gillies. Lillie was to become not only Gillies's most important patron (by the time of his death he owned a total of 372 works by Gillies, out of a collection of over 600 pictures) but also his most active supporter, encouraging critics to review Gillies's work and lending his own collection for public exhibition. In 1949 Gillies held the first of many, regular one-man exhibitions at The Scottish Gallery. His work was shown in London in 1951 at the Festival of Britain on the South Bank, and again in 1954, this time more extensively in a joint exhibition with John Maxwell organised by the Arts Council and held at the New Burlington Galleries. On his return to Scotland Gillies wrote on a postcard to Lillie:

We got back at 6.15 yesterday and I left John at Waverley, seeking bk-fast in the N.B. [North British Hotel] *A very pleasant holiday – glad you were there ... It is just as cold and dreary up here as it was in London – yesterday here was even worse. I went on bike over to Gladhouse and there were still snow drifts at sides of road.*[26]

Gillies was of a modest nature and did not enjoy the public exposure that exhibitions of his work brought. In spite of his complaint about the weather there is a sense of relief in this note to Lillie at being back in the Border countryside. Although expeditions around Scotland continued throughout the 1950s and 1960s and into the 1970s (Lillie was to receive postcards from Fyvie, in Aberdeenshire, in 1971, and from the Mull of Kintyre in 1972), it was the Border countryside that dominated Gillies's subject-matter and it is for his studies of it in oil, watercolour and pencil that he remains most publicly known. In *March, Moorfoot* [plate 21], a view looking south across Gladhouse Reservoir to the Moorfoot Hills, Gillies reduces his palette to monochromes of grey and black. The clarity with which he conveys the lingering winter aspect of this March scene, leaving the paper untouched to indicate the late snow lying in the gullies, makes it one of his masterpieces. Gillies commented on his work of the 1950s and 1960s: 'I believe I am now achieving a simplicity I have striven for, for a long, long time'.[27] This quality of simplicity in Gillies's late landscape work is, as his comment suggests,

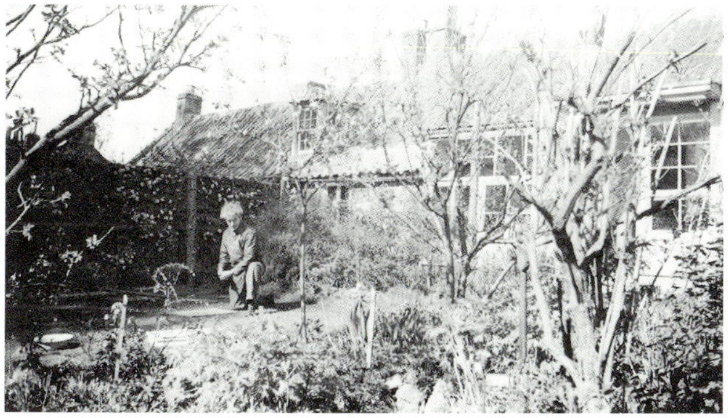

Gillies working in his garden, Temple, 1960s

deceptive and belies the skill he developed over a long career in discerning the essential spirit of his subject. If his landscape painting can seem on occasion unassuming, it is because he had no desire to impose on his subject an epic or deliberately picturesque quality but sought to communicate as directly and simply as he could its fundamental nature.

I would plead that in landscape [painting] *I have perhaps opened to many peoples' eyes, some unexpected, some subtle beauty in our daily surroundings. This has been I hope a by-product of my own enjoyment of what I perceive and my great delight in the very act of handling paint.*[28]

His ability to reveal, without pretence, the subtle beauty of the Scottish landscape sets him aside as one of its greatest painters.

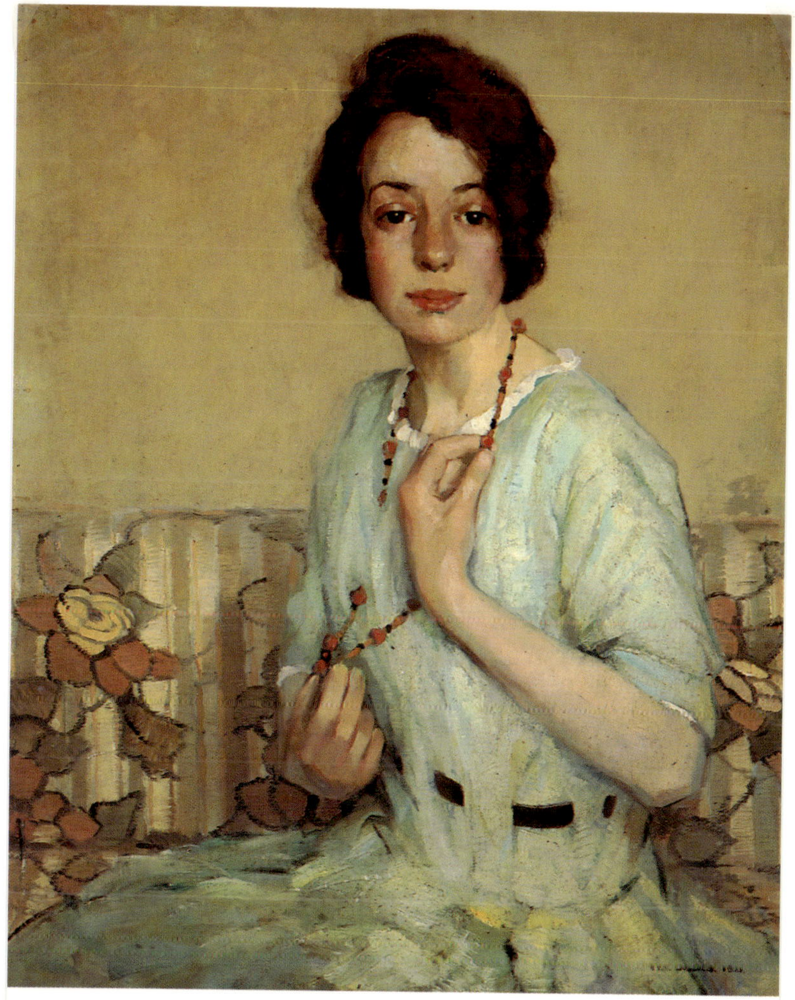

Portrait of Emma Gillies (1921)

NOTES

1 Thomas Elder Dickson, *W. G. Gillies*, Edinburgh University Press, 1974, p.5.

2 'W. G. Gillies: the Artist Reminiscences' in *The Christian Science Monitor*, 12 March 1970. Among Gillies's material bequeathed to the Royal Scottish Academy is a group of sketch-books containing drawings made while in the trenches.

3 Edinburgh College of Art, *Prospectus for Session 1919–20*. The staff of the College's School of Drawing and Painting comprised, for that session: William Walls, John Menzies, Henry J. Lintott (Teacher of Anatomy), David M. Sutherland, Walter G. Grieve, Adam B. Thomson (Teacher of Etching), Donald Moodie, Annie Morgan, Dorothy Johnstone, Dorothy Nesbitt, Dorothy Thorburn, and Robert F. Sherar (Teacher of Geometry and Perspective).

4 *ibid.*

5 Elder Dickson gives a date of 1920 for this award and that Gillies travelled to London in the Easter vacation. Gillies's official student report records that he was 'Awarded a Minor Travelling Bursary of £20 – Summer 1921'. I am grateful to Katrina Thomson of the Edinburgh College of Art for this information.

6 *Catalogue of the First Exhibition of the Society of Scottish Artists*, Edinburgh 1892.

7 The founding members of the 1922 Group, in addition to Gillies, were Arthur Couling, William Geissler, William Crozier, David Gunn, George Hall, William MacTaggart, Alexander Munro and George Watson.

8 Edinburgh College of Art, *Prospectus for Session 1922–23*.

9 Elder Dickson, *op.cit.* p.20.

10 Geissler later became Head of the Art Department at the teacher training college Moray House, Edinburgh.

11 *The Christian Science Monitor*, *op. cit.*

12 Letter to Dr R. A. Lillie, 1960, on deposit at the National Library of Scotland, deposit number 316/4f.

13 W. E. Johnston, 'The Compleat Man', *The Manchester Guardian*, 7 May 1961.

14 *Catalogue of the Society of Scottish Artists*, *op. cit.*

15 The works exhibited by Munch are listed in the 1931 SSA catalogue as; *Woman in Red*, *The Waves*, *Winter Landscape*, *Landscape*, *The Bathers*, *Bohemian Wedding*, *Lady in Grey*, *Melancholy*, *Landscape*, *The Forest*, *Galloping Horse*, *Nude*.

16 In 1892 Munch had been invited to participate at the annual exhibition of the Verein Berliner Kunstler (Society of Berlin Artists). The resulting controversy caused by his work led to a split among the Society with a group resigning and forming the Berlin Secession.

17 Elder Dickson, *op. cit.* p.25.

18 *ibid.* p.26.

19 *ibid.* p.66.

20 David McClure, *John Maxwell*, Edinburgh University Press, 1976, p.17.

21 *The Christian Science Monitor*, *op. cit.*

22 Postcard to Mrs E. Gillies, 1951, Gillies Bequest, Royal Scottish Academy.

23 Postcard to Dr R. A. Lillie, 1951, on deposit at the National Library of Scotland, deposit number 316/4f.

24 Postcard to Dr R. A. Lillie, on deposit at the National Library of Scotland, deposit number 316/4f.

25 George Scott-Moncrieff, 'Fresh Aspects of Beauty', *The Times Educational Supplement*, 6 February 1970.

26 Postcard to Dr R. A. Lillie, 15 March 1954, on deposit at the National Library of Scotland, deposit number 316/4f.

27 *Still Life with Honesty*: a film on Gillies's life and work produced by OGAM Films for the Scottish Arts Council, 1969.

28 *ibid.*

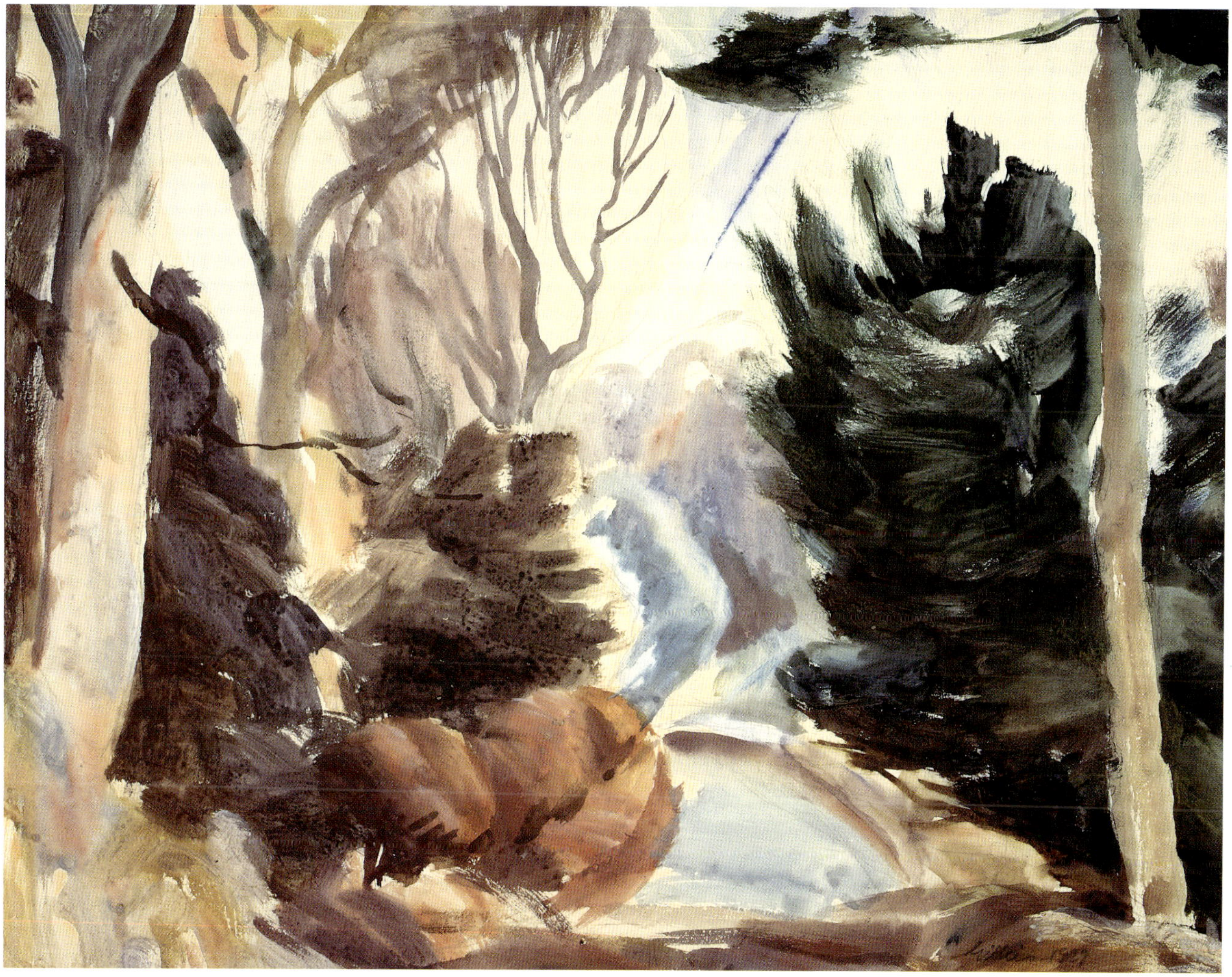

1 WOODLAND PATH
dated 1926 · catalogue 1

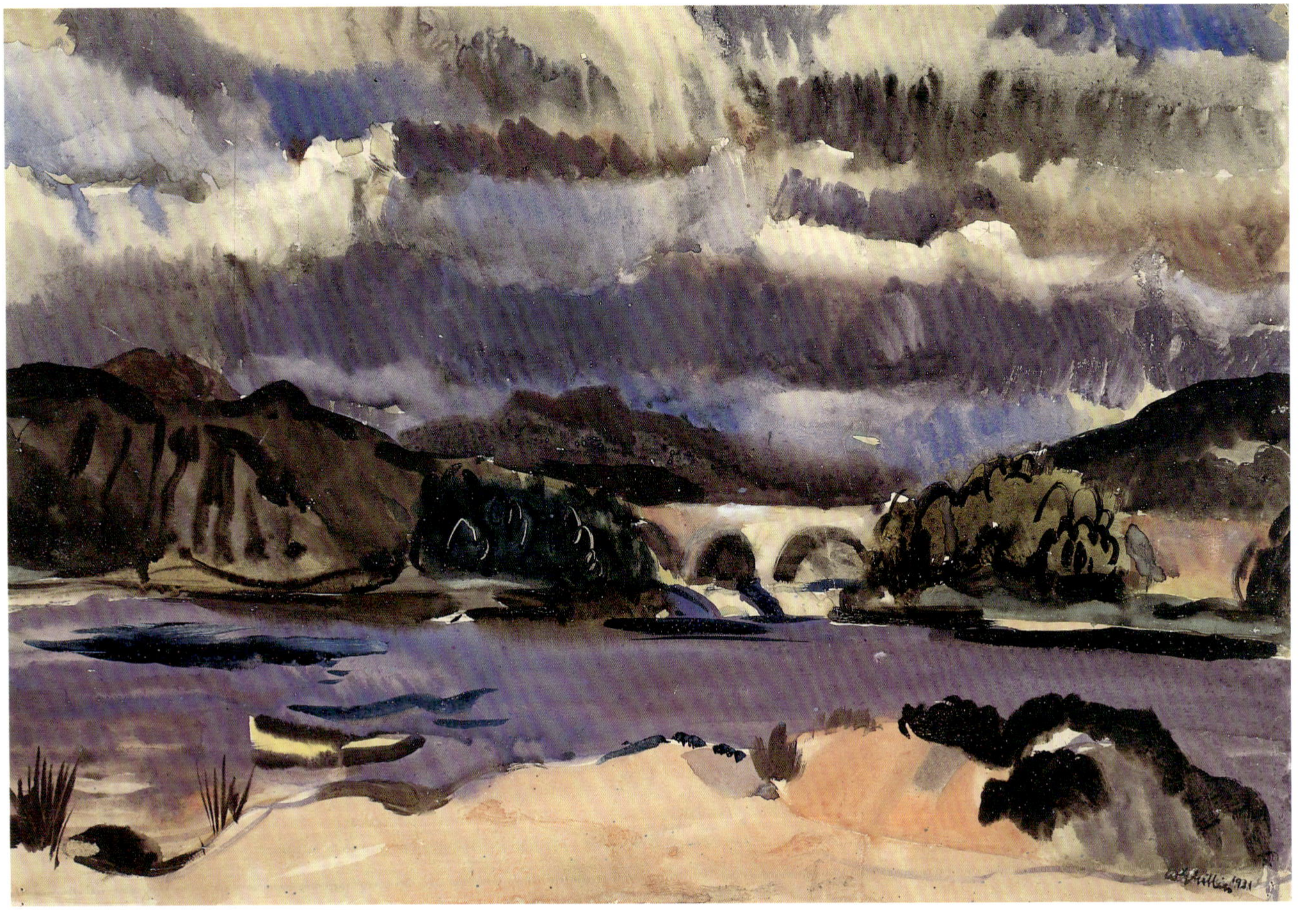

2 MORAR
dated 1931 · catalogue 4

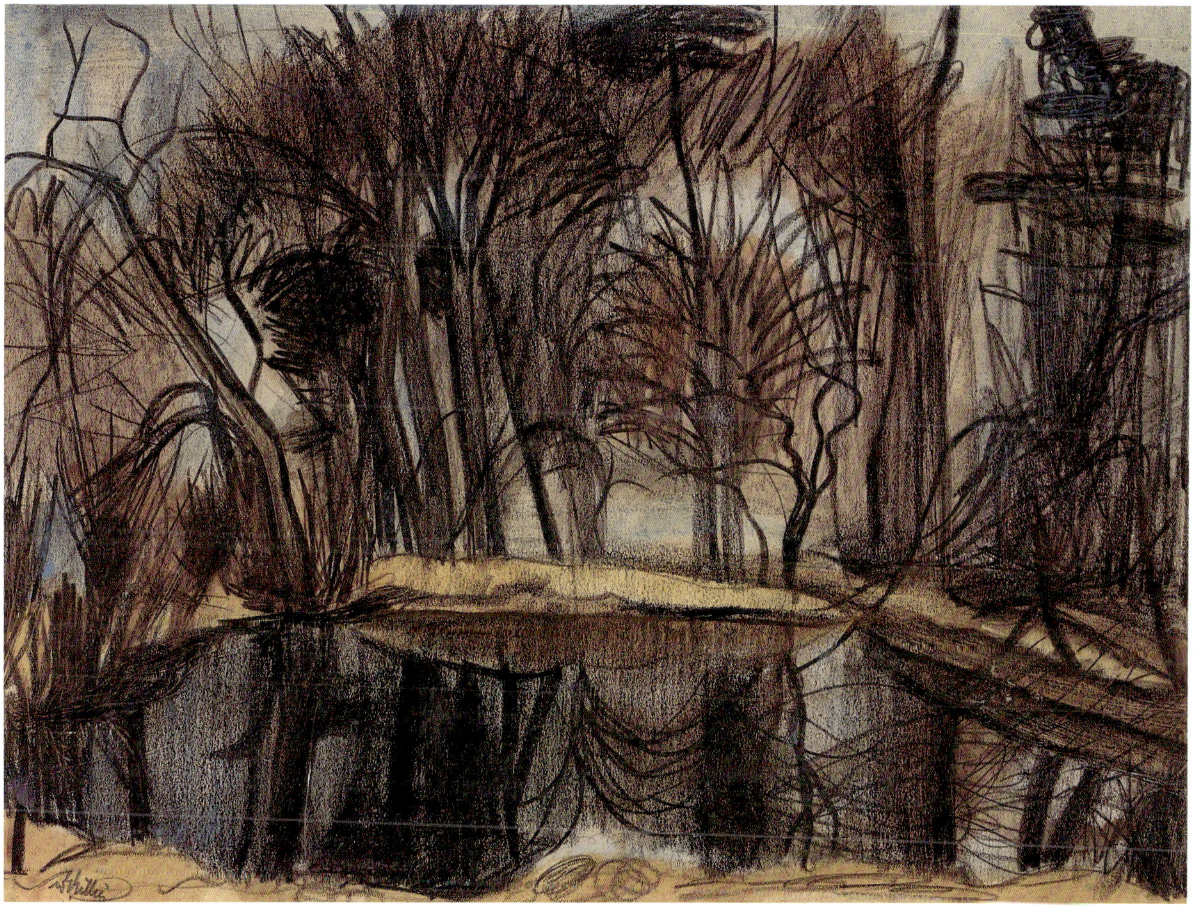

3 A POOL
dated 1932 · catalogue 6

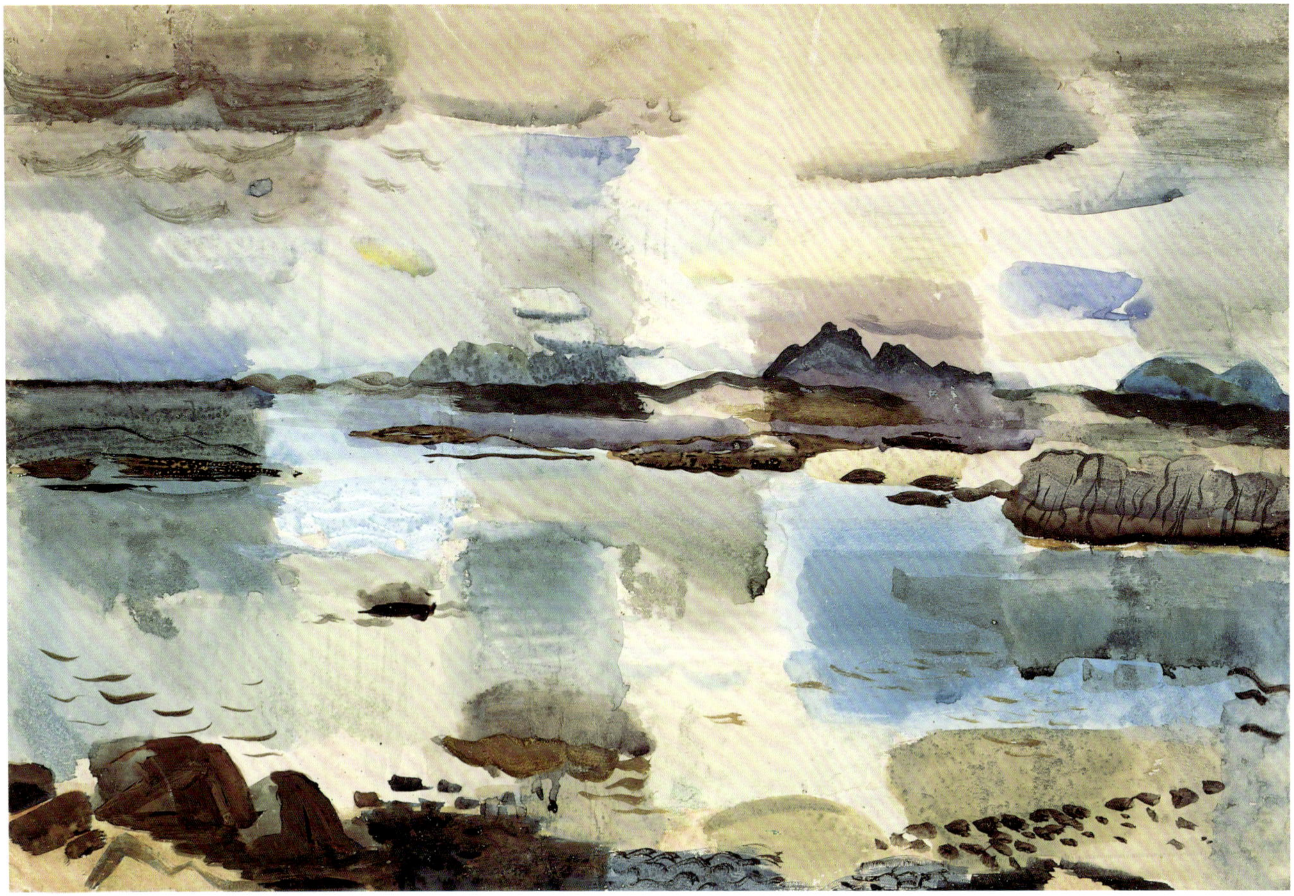

above

4 SKYE HILLS FROM NEAR MORAR
circa 1931 · catalogue 5

opposite

5 IN ARDNAMURCHAN
circa 1936 · catalogue 11

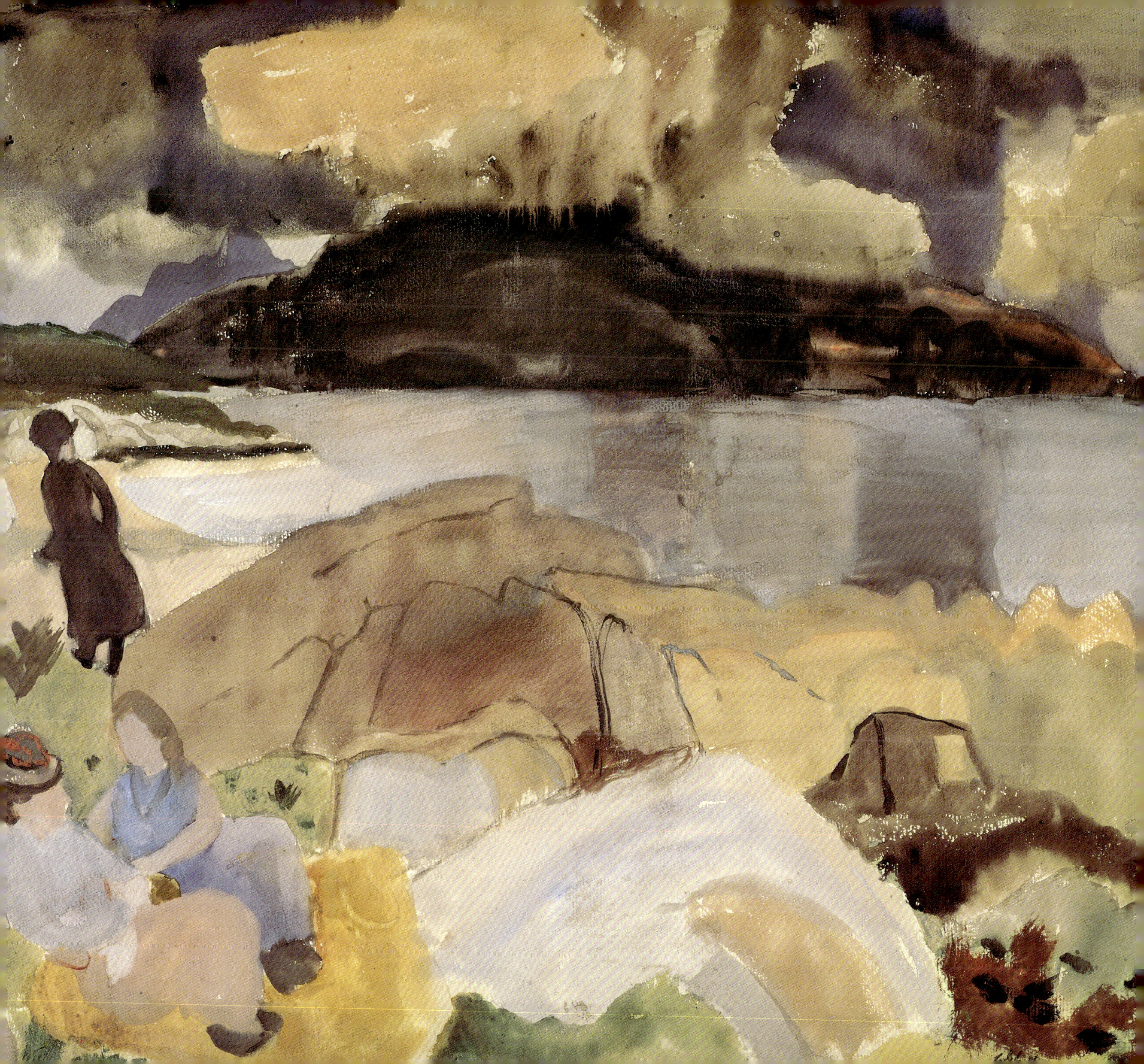

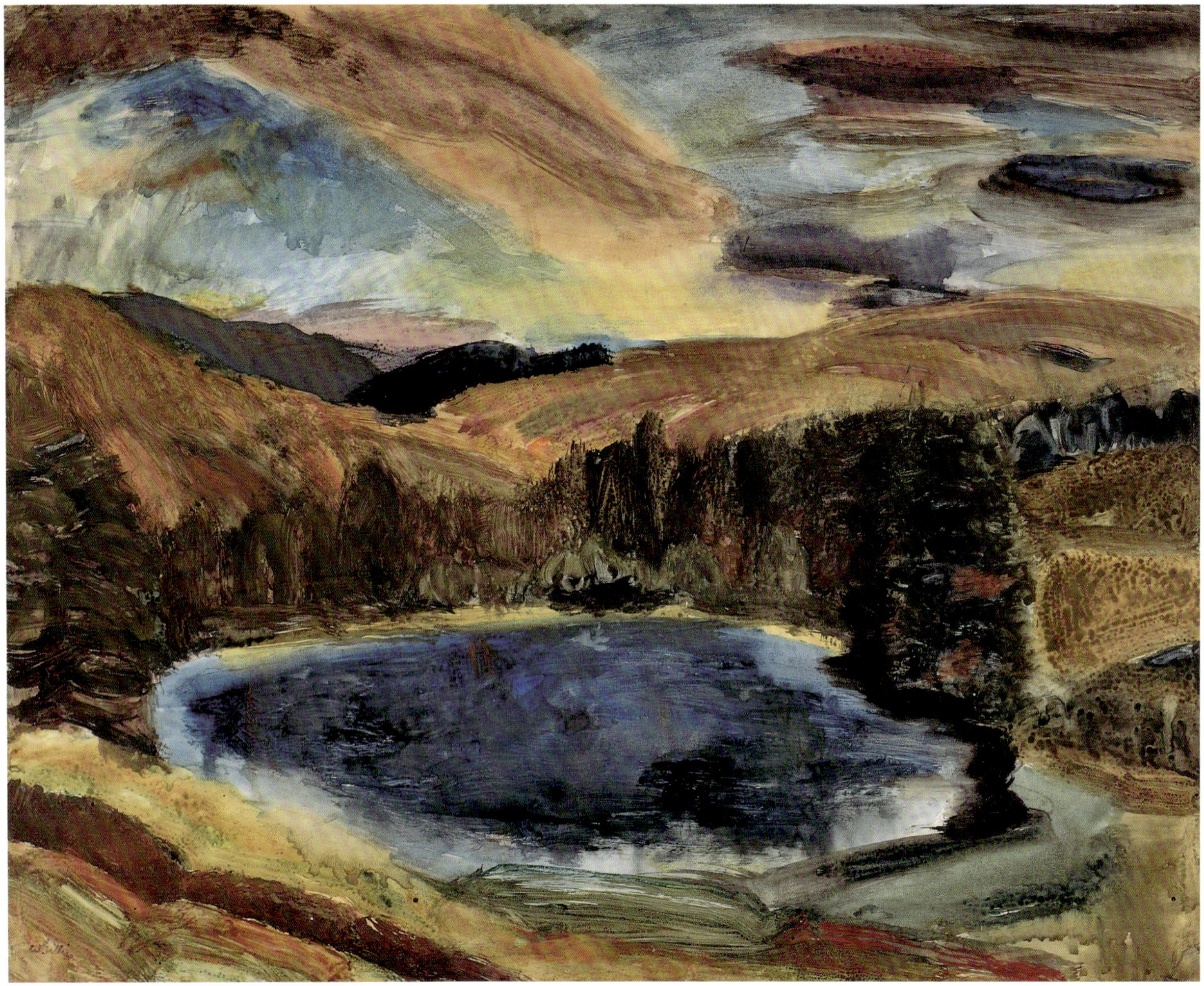

6 THE DARK POND
circa 1934 · catalogue 9

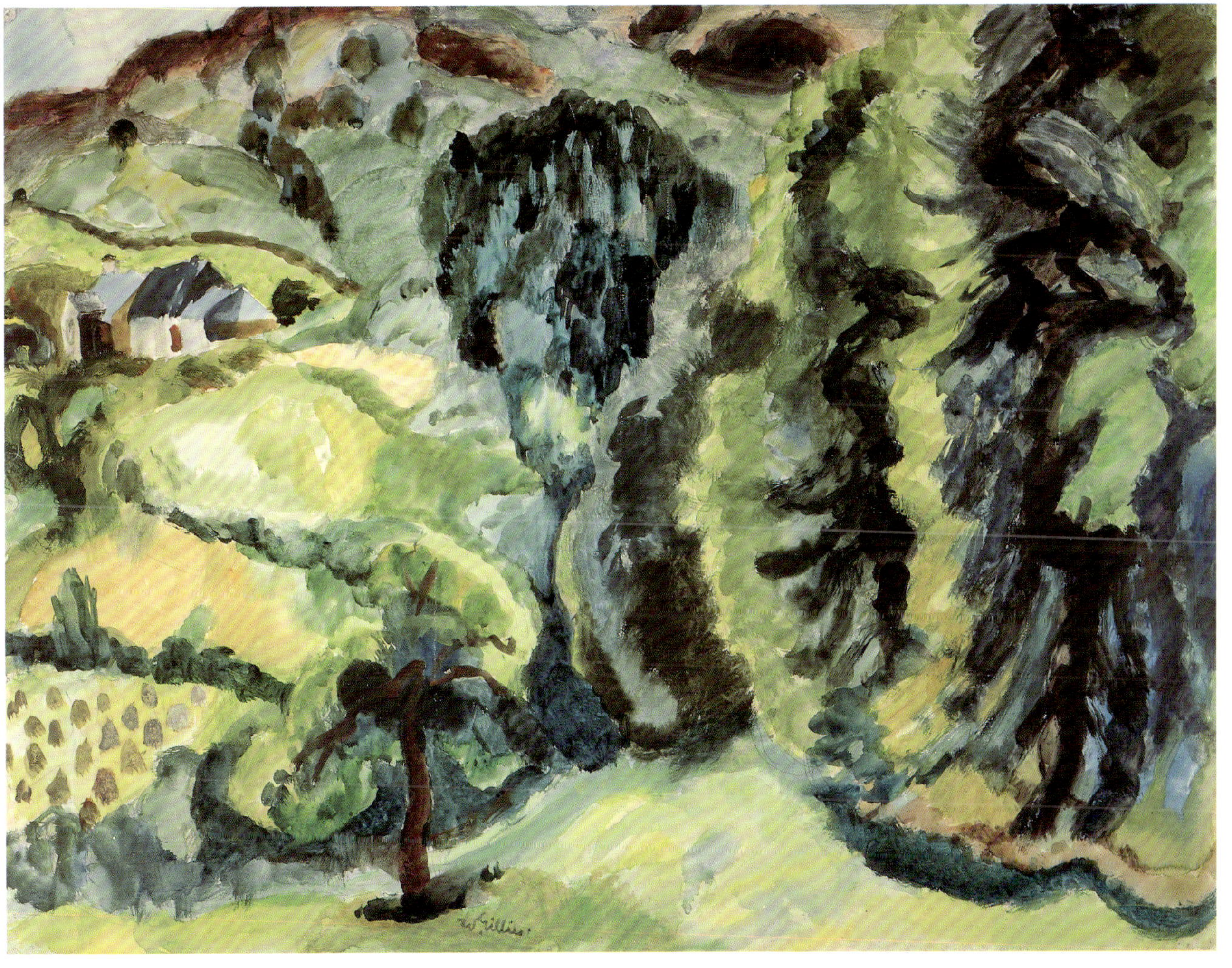

7 HEAD OF THE GLEN
mid – late 1930s · catalogue 10

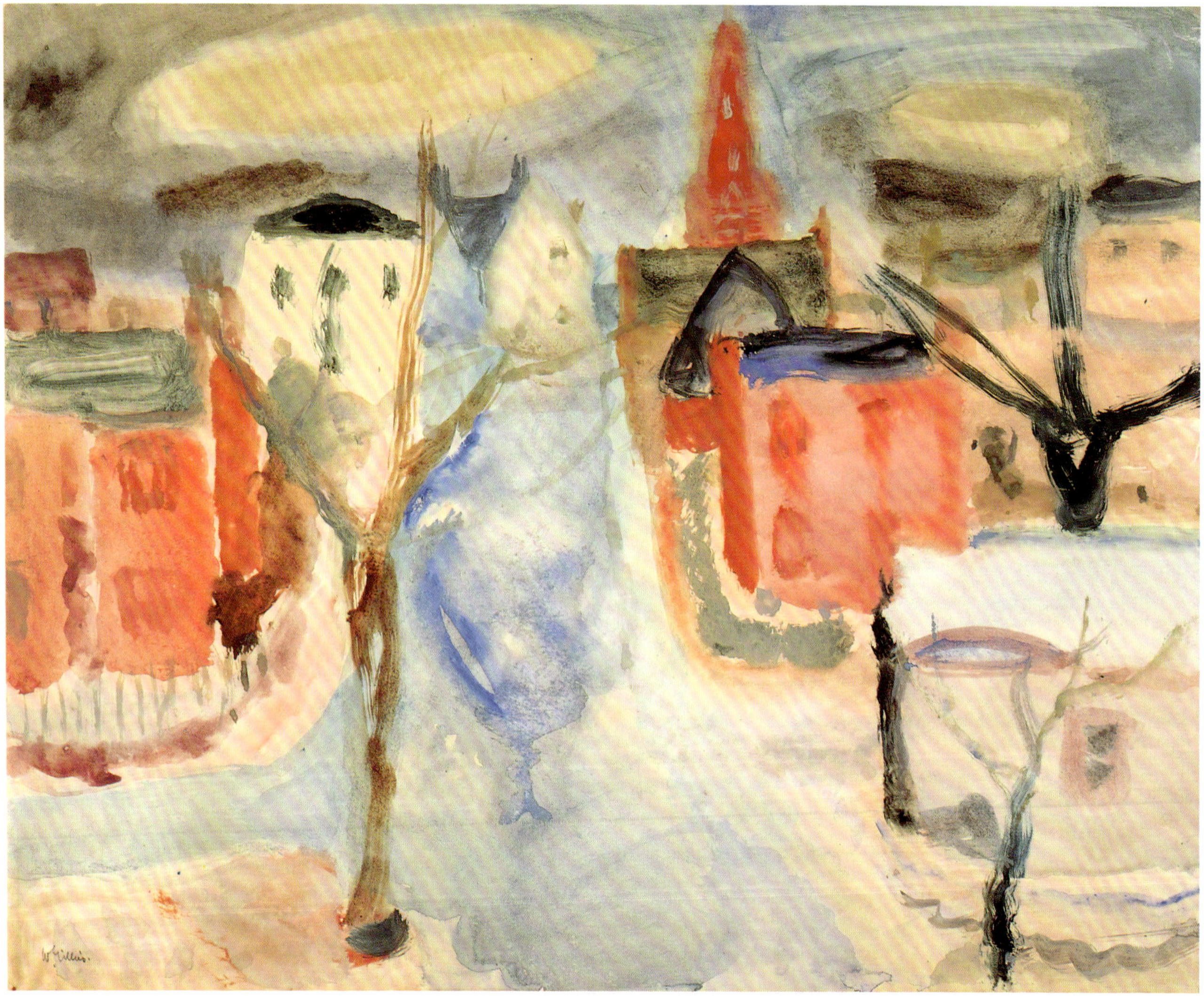

8 THE STREET
circa 1933 · catalogue 8

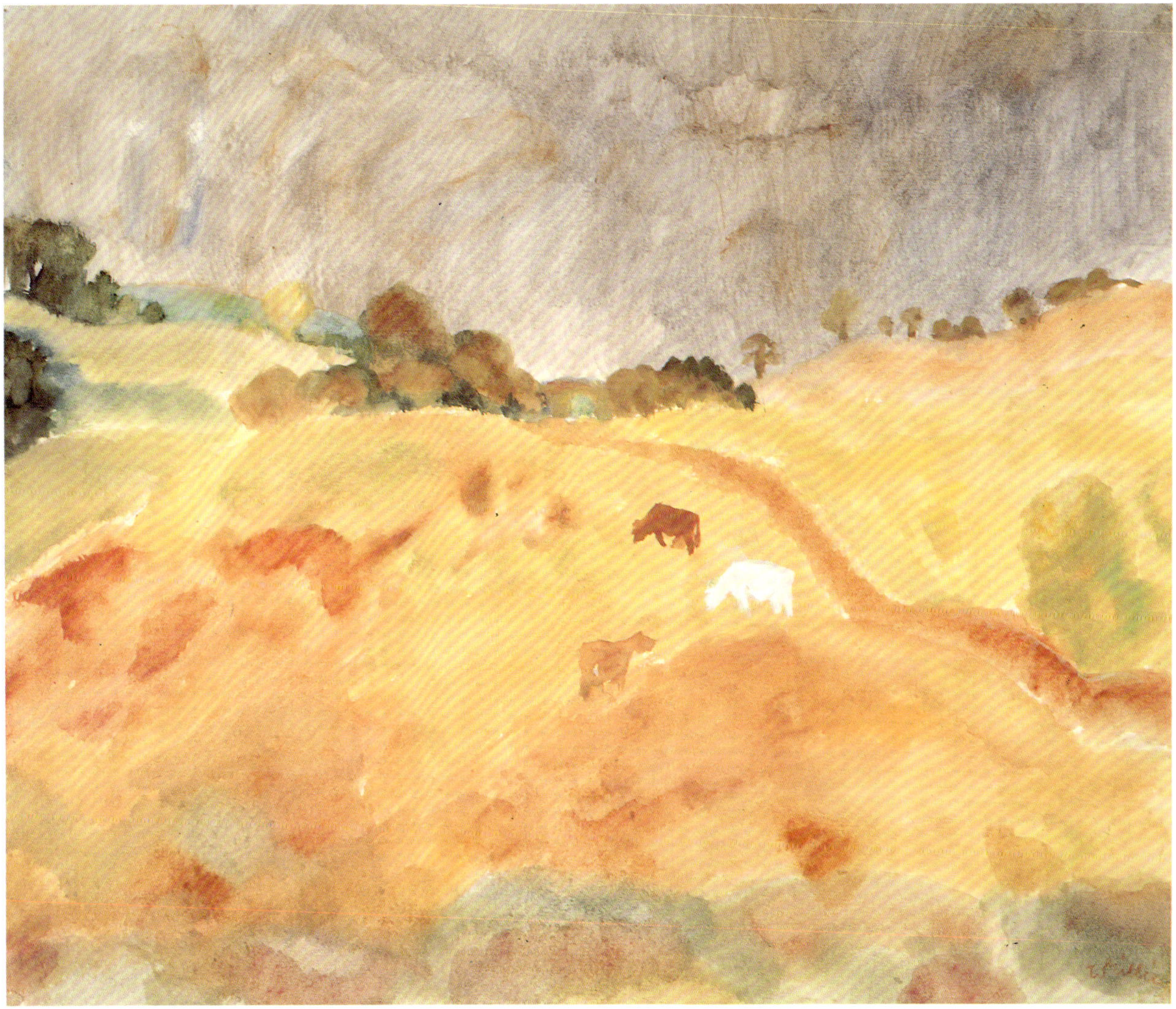

9 CASTLETON
circa 1944 · catalogue 21

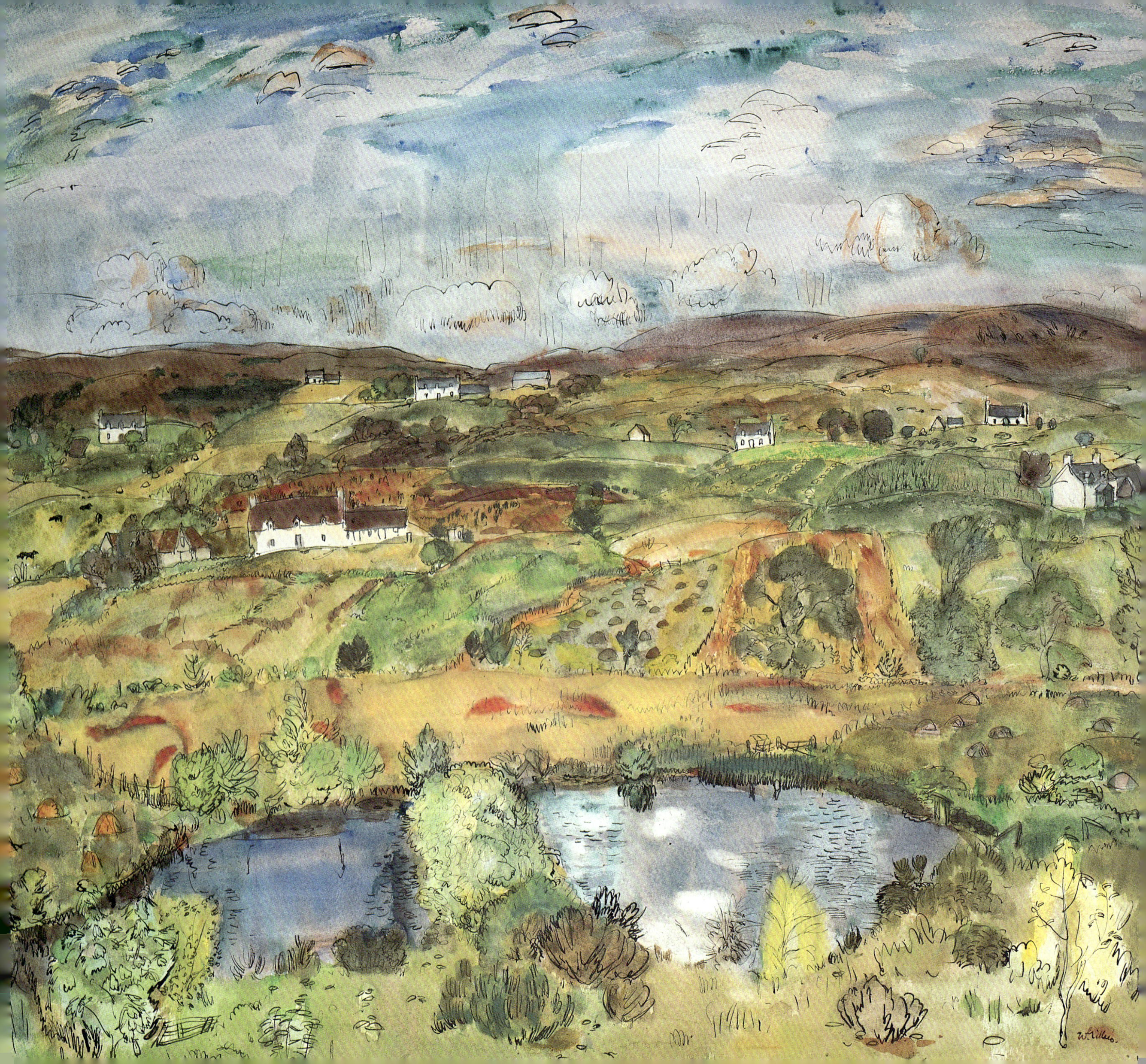

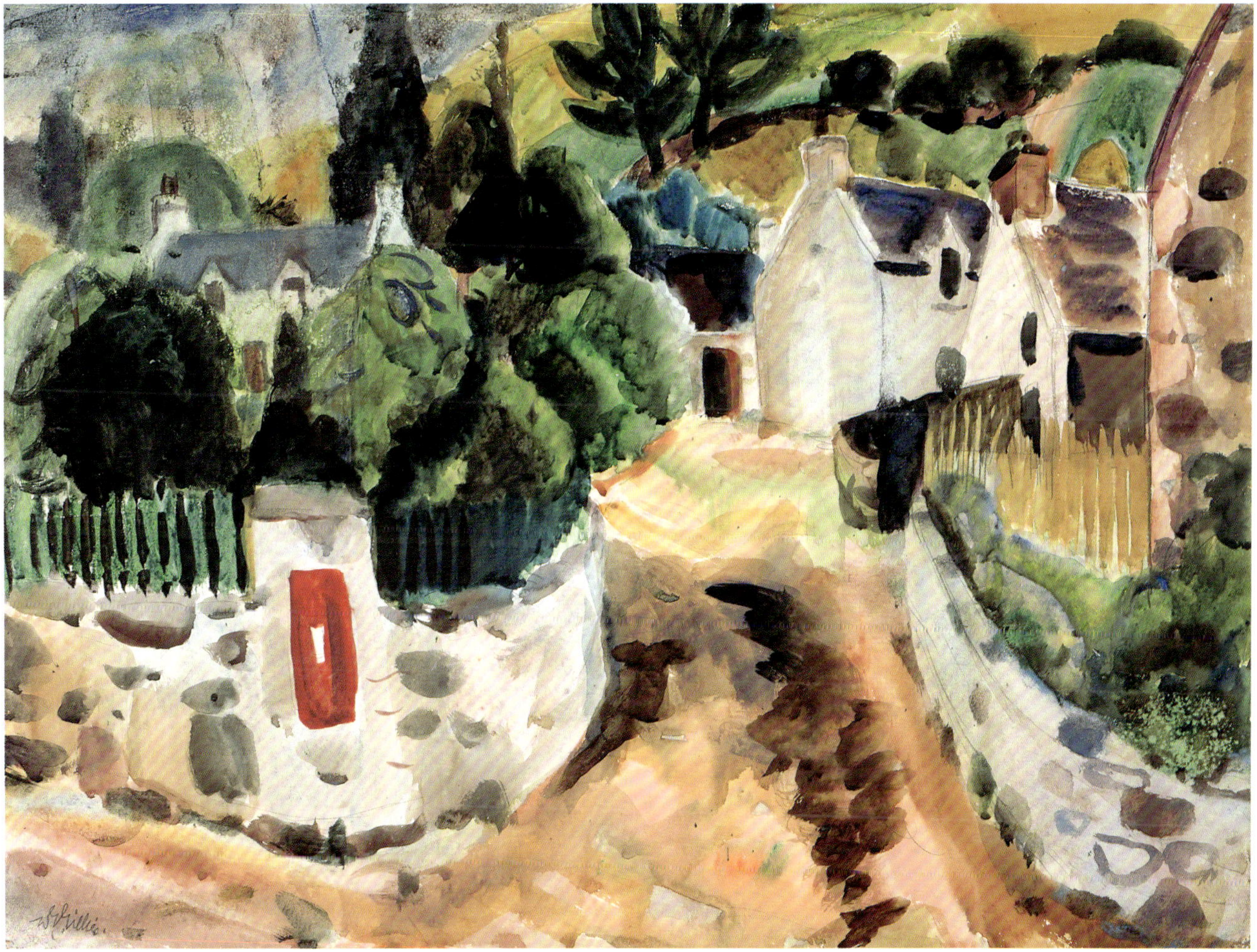

opposite

10 CROFTS, BONAR BRIDGE
circa 1938 · catalogue 16

above

11 THE VILLAGE LETTER BOX
1940s · catalogue 18

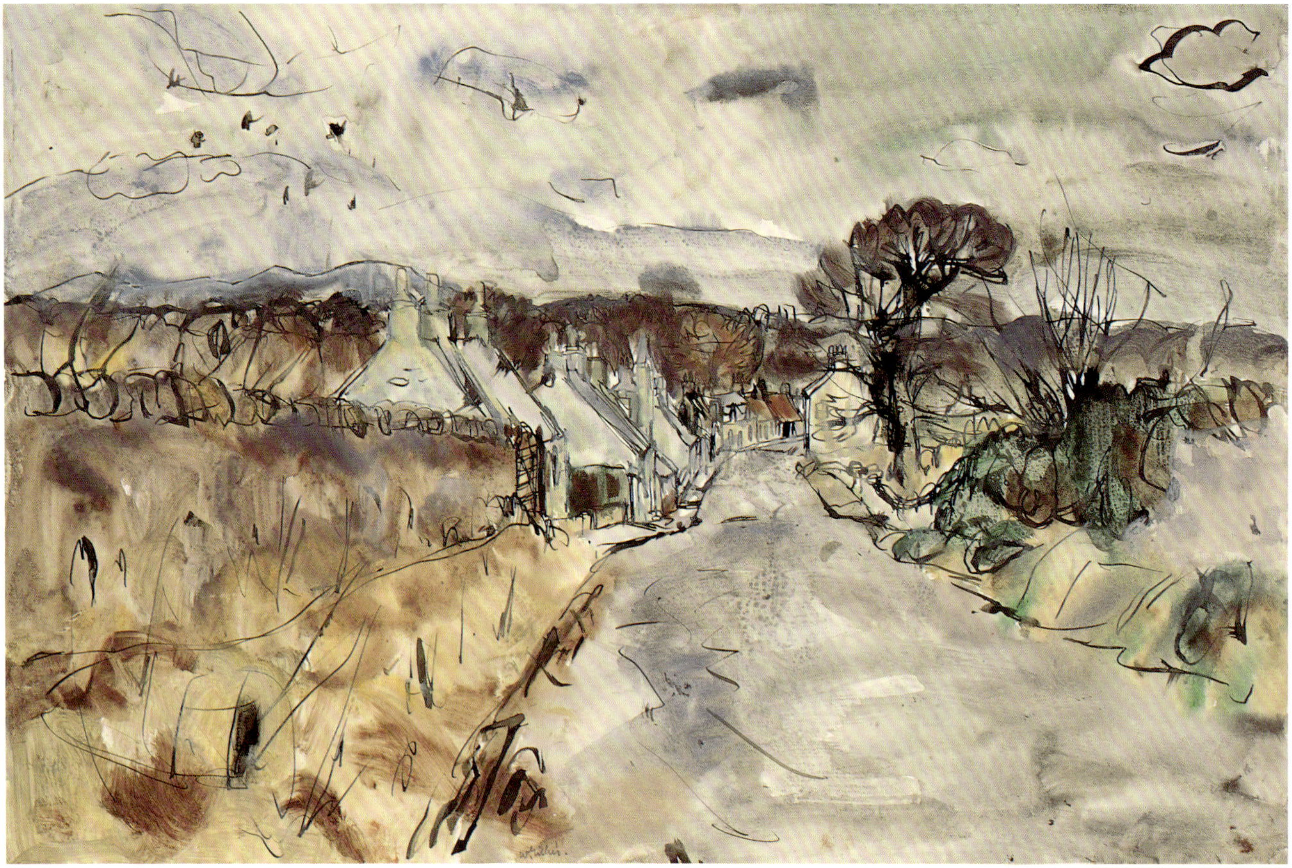

above

12 WINTER AFTERNOON, TEMPLE
circa 1942 · catalogue 20

opposite

13 THE POND
circa 1945–48 · catalogue 24

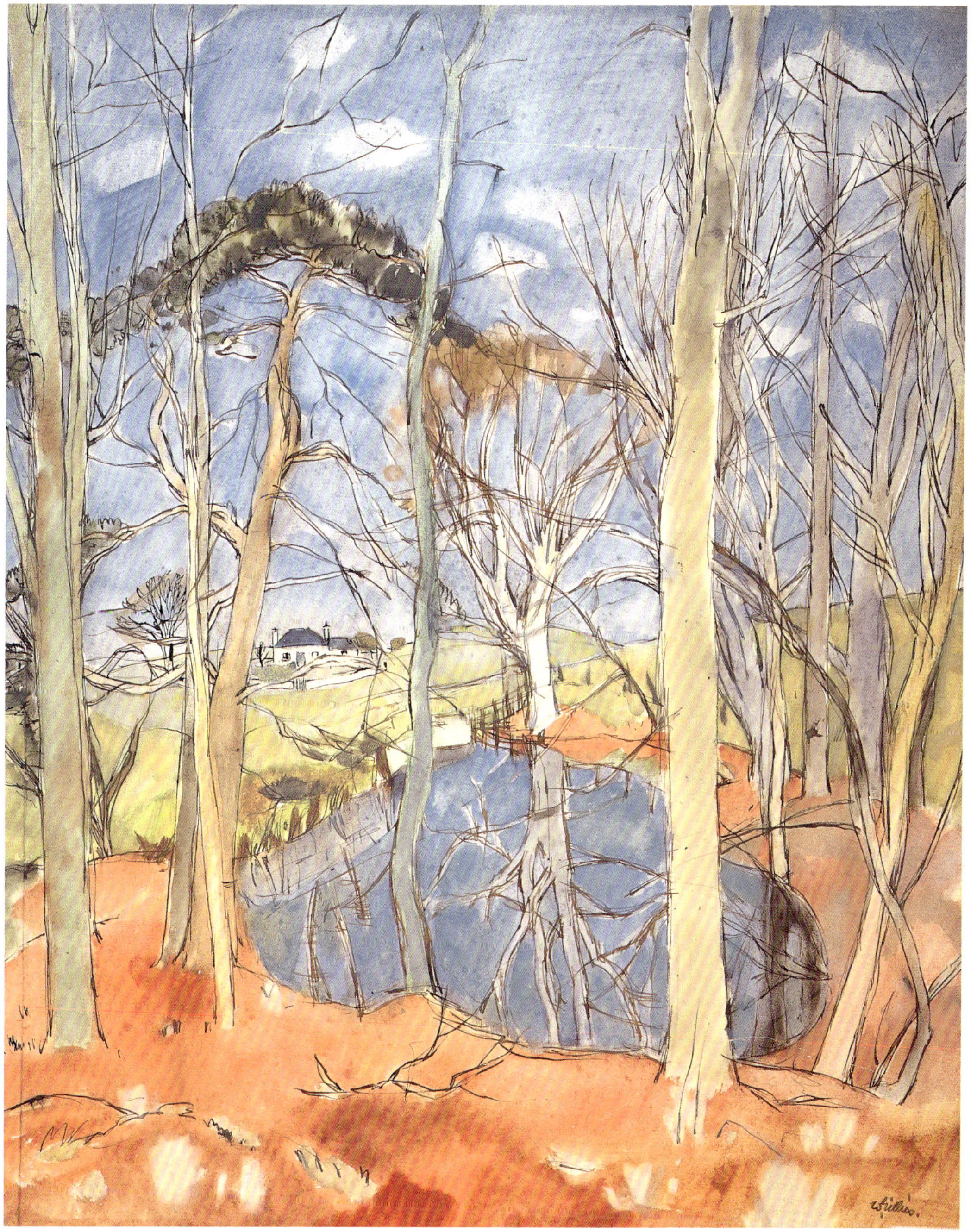

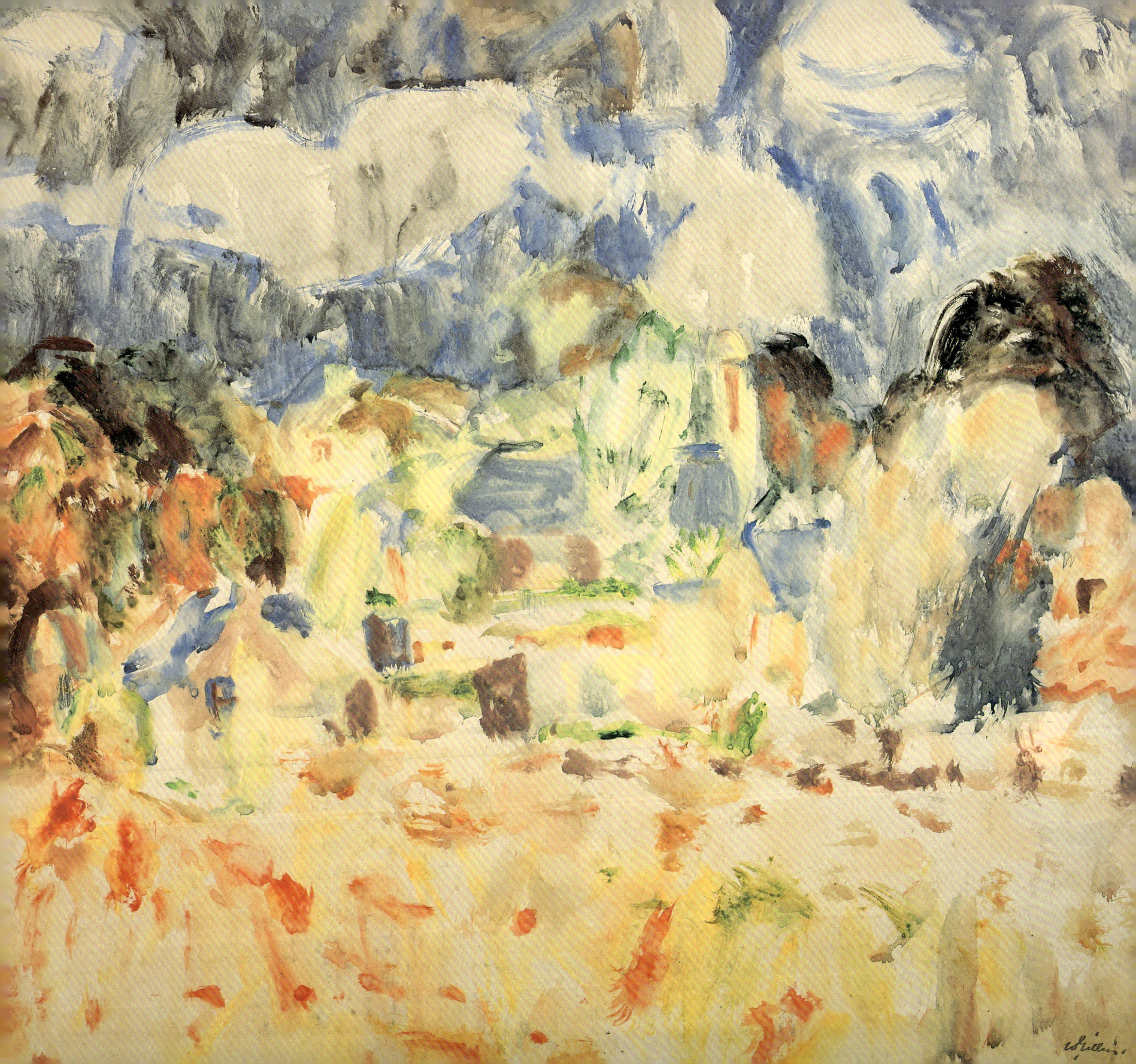

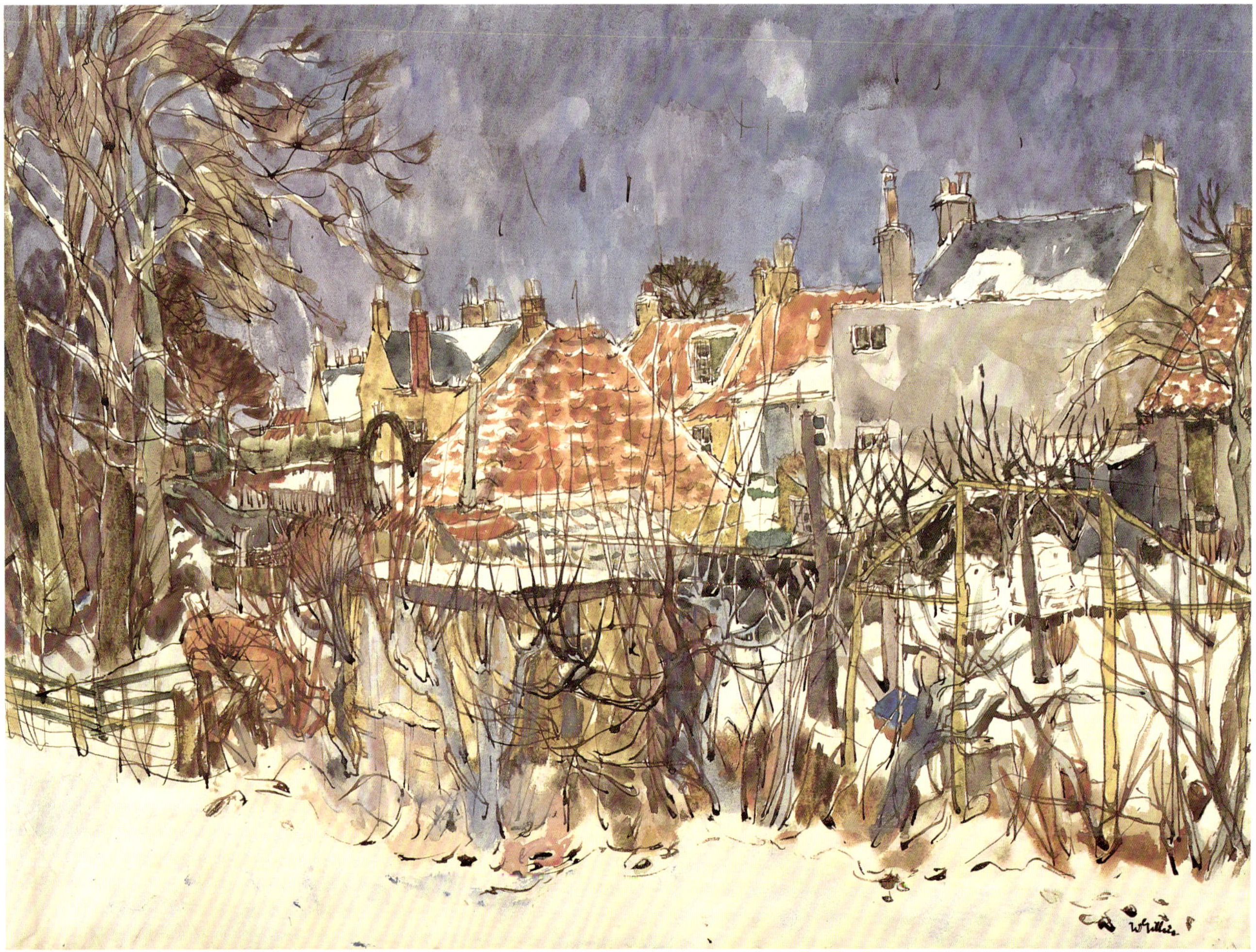

opposite

14 LANDSCAPE WITH HOUSES, TEMPLE
mid-1940s · catalogue 23

above

15 WINTER, TEMPLE (BACK OF HOUSES)
circa 1949 · catalogue 46

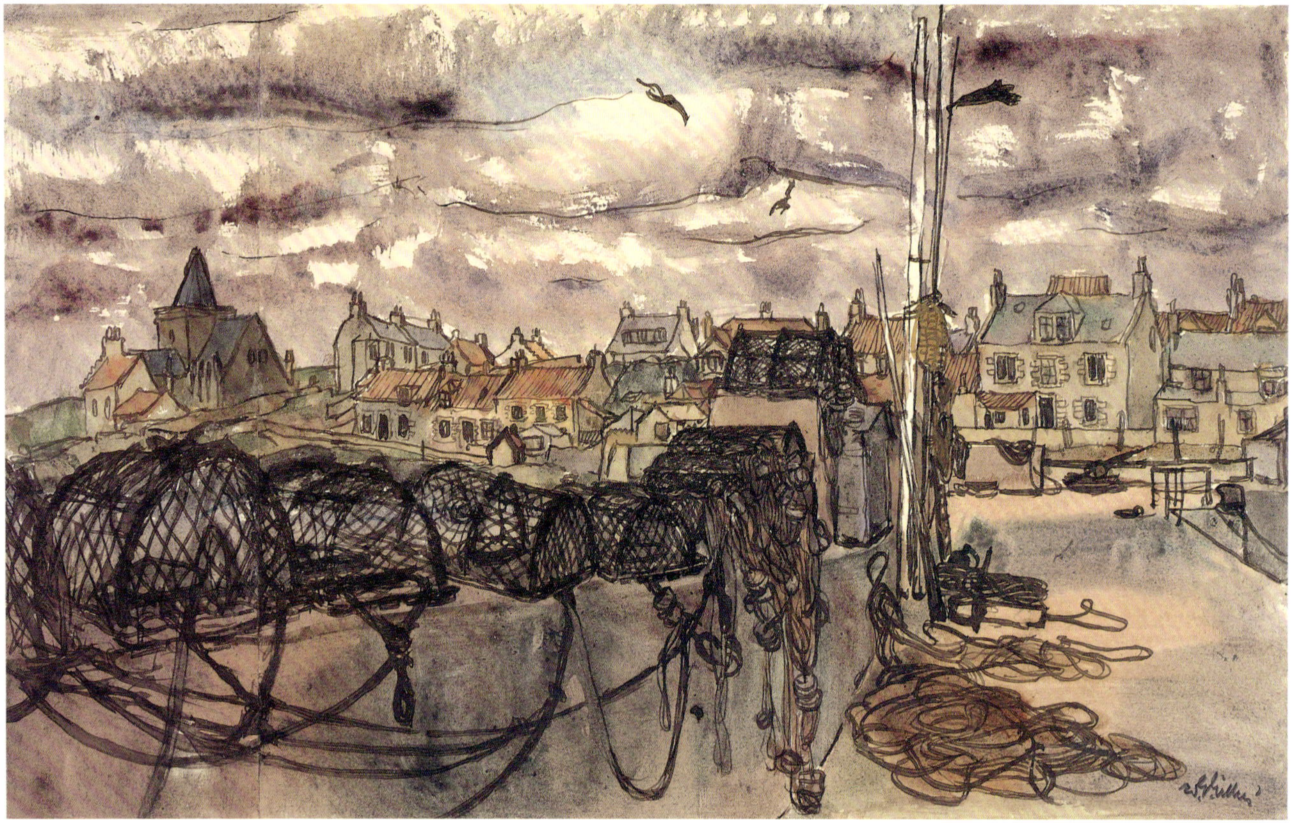

16 ST MONANCE FROM THE HARBOUR
circa 1949 · catalogue 45

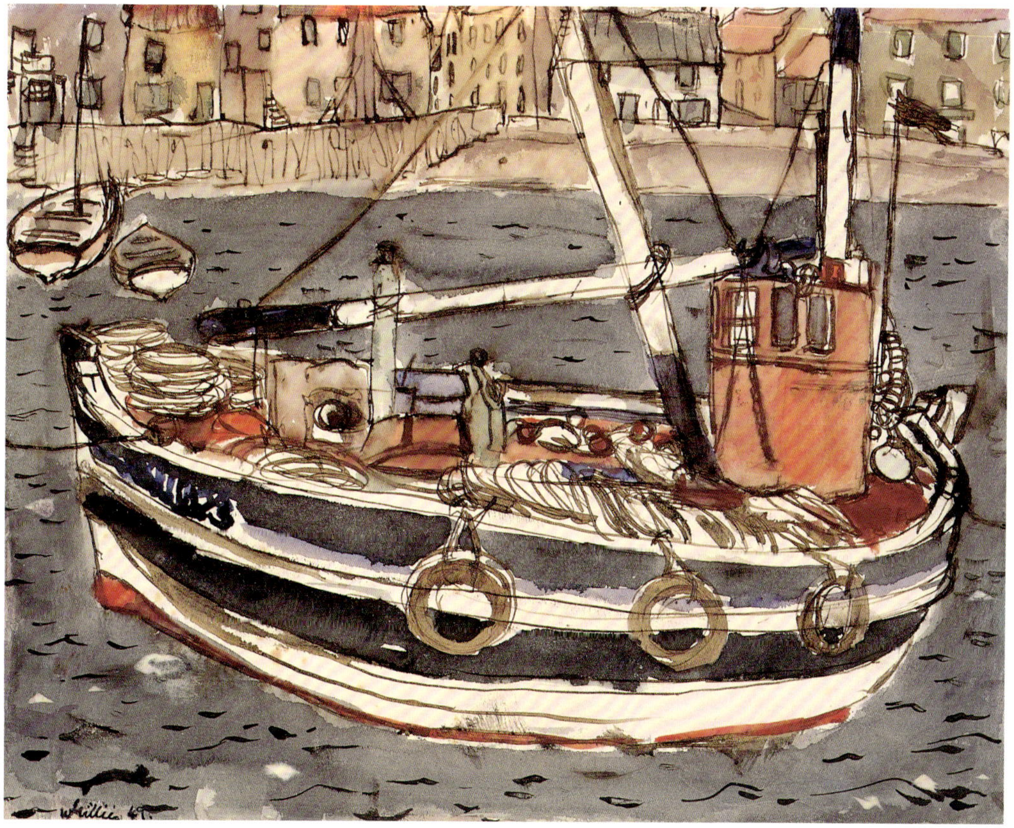

17 THE FISHING BOAT
dated 1949 · catalogue 42

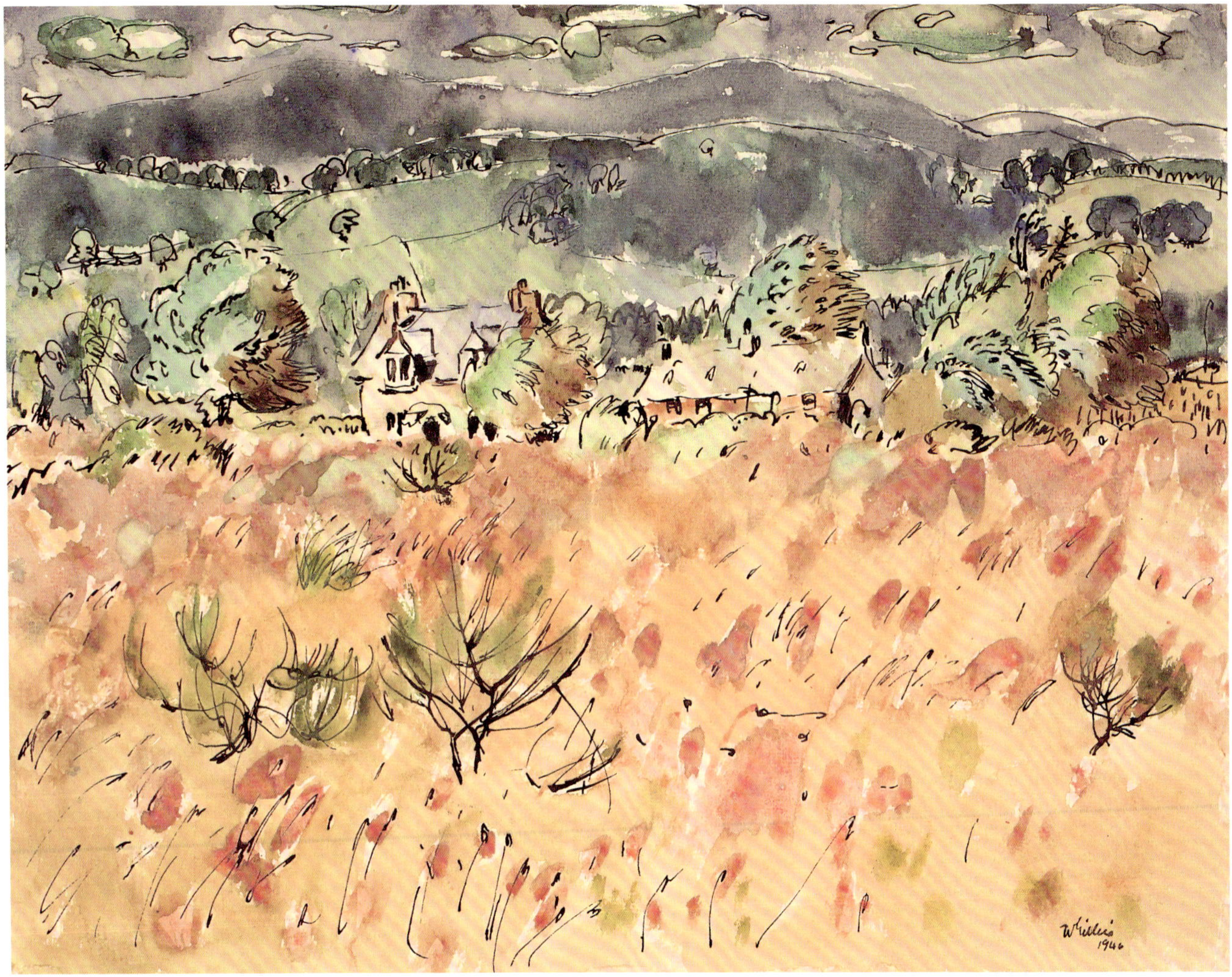

18 WIND ABOVE KIRRIEMUIR
dated 1946 · catalogue 31

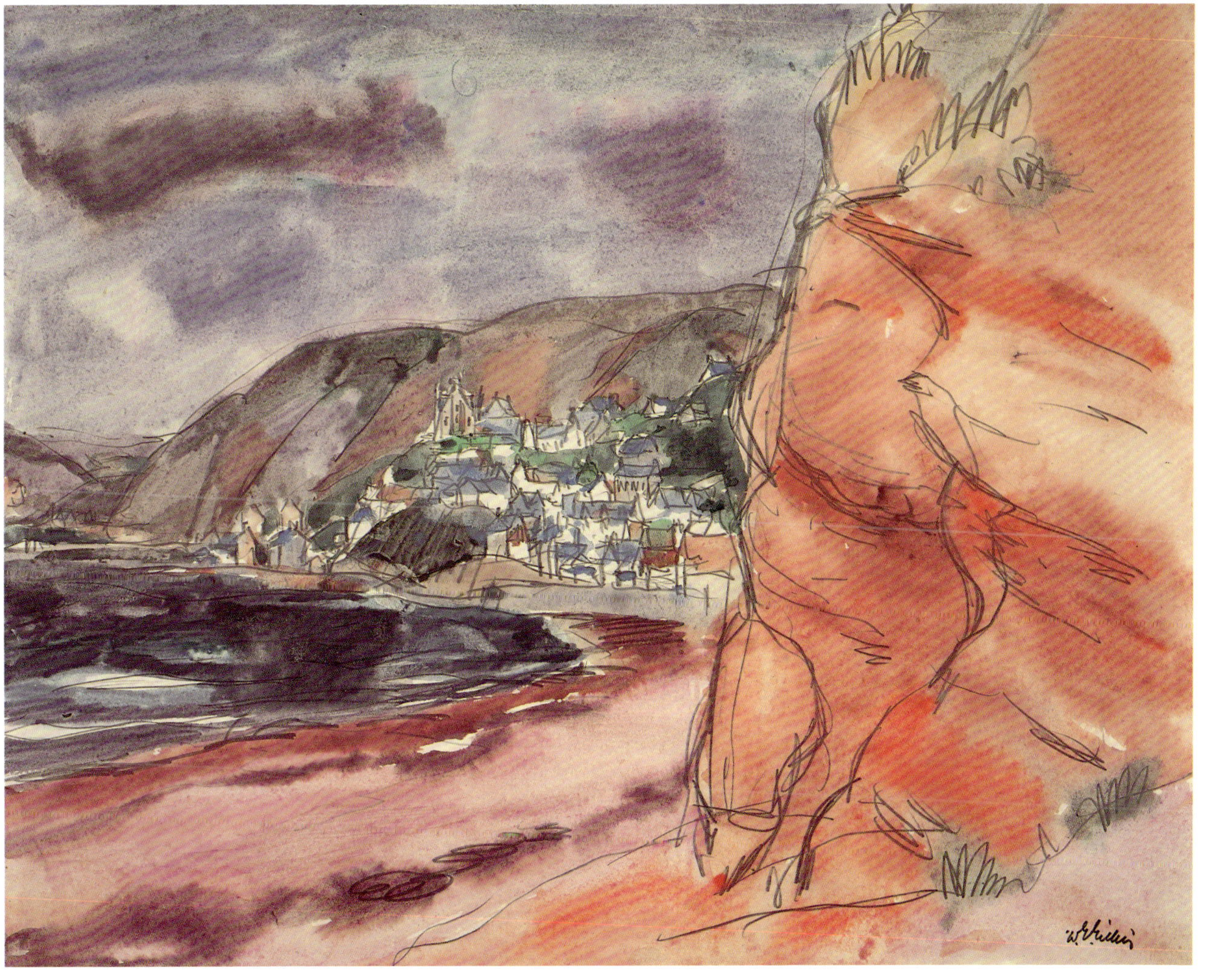

19 GARDENSTOWN – RED CLIFF
circa 1950 · catalogue 48

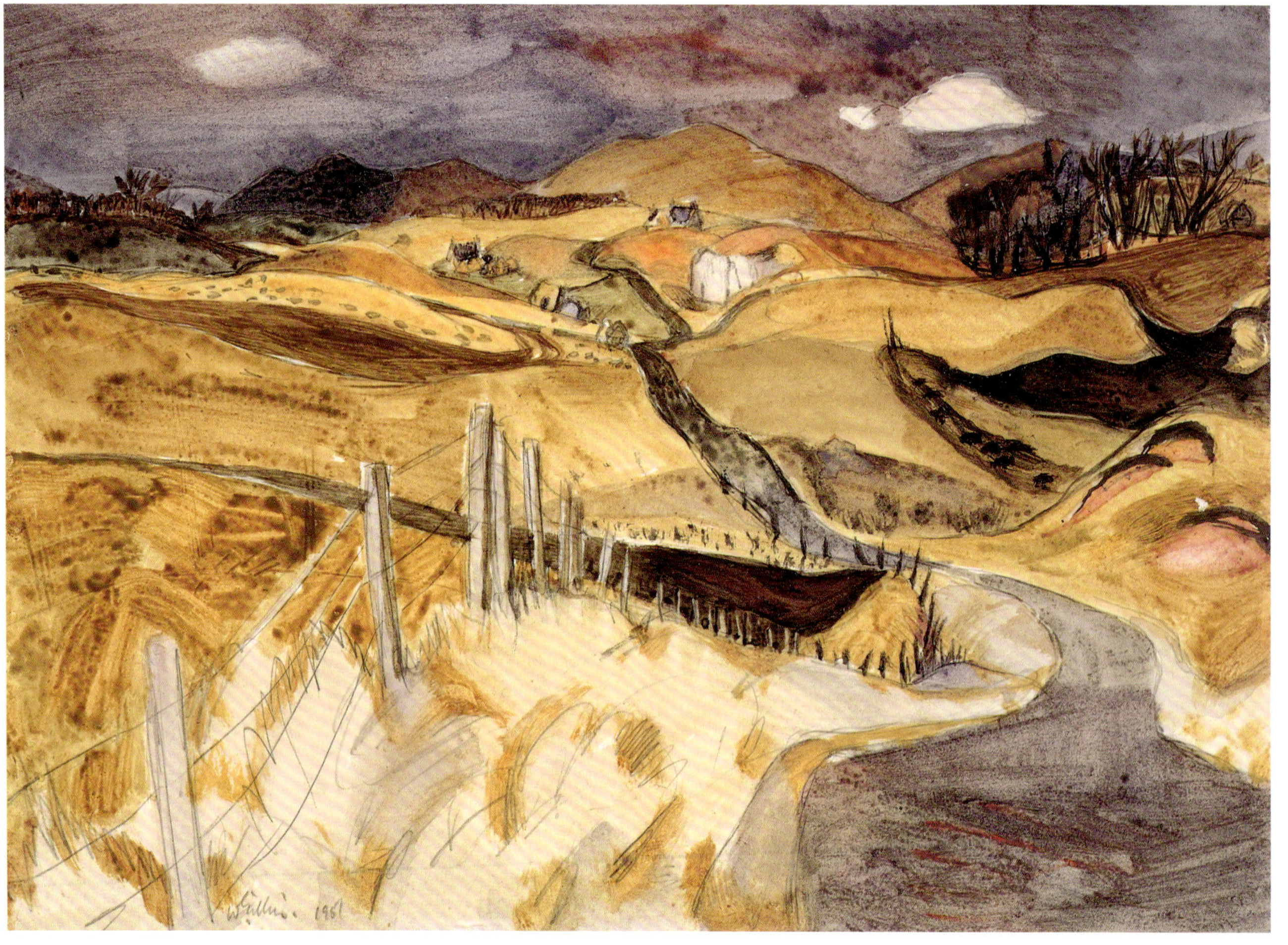

above

20 NEAR HOWGATE
dated 1951 · catalogue 54

opposite

21 MARCH, MOORFOOT
dated 1951 · catalogue 56

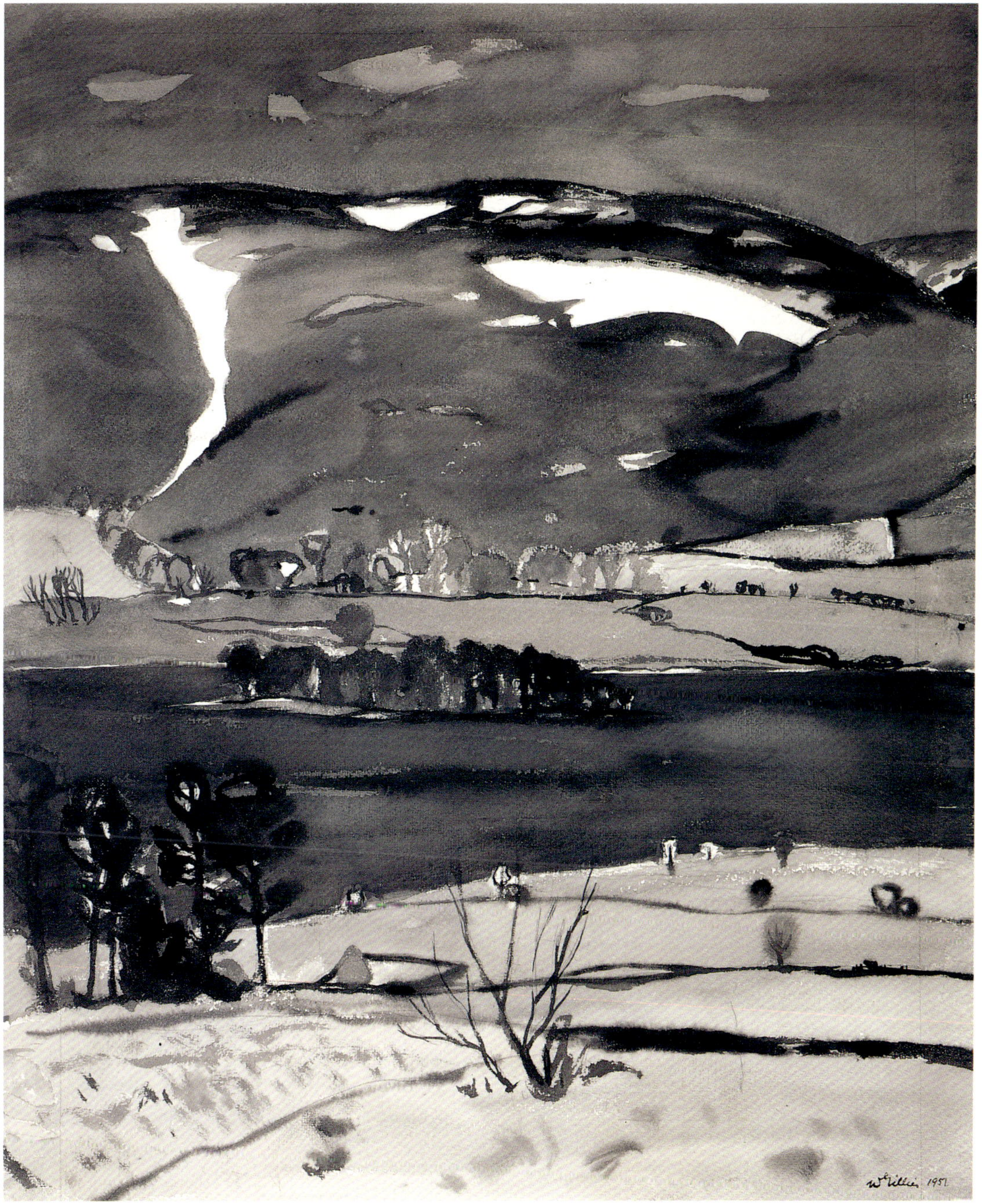

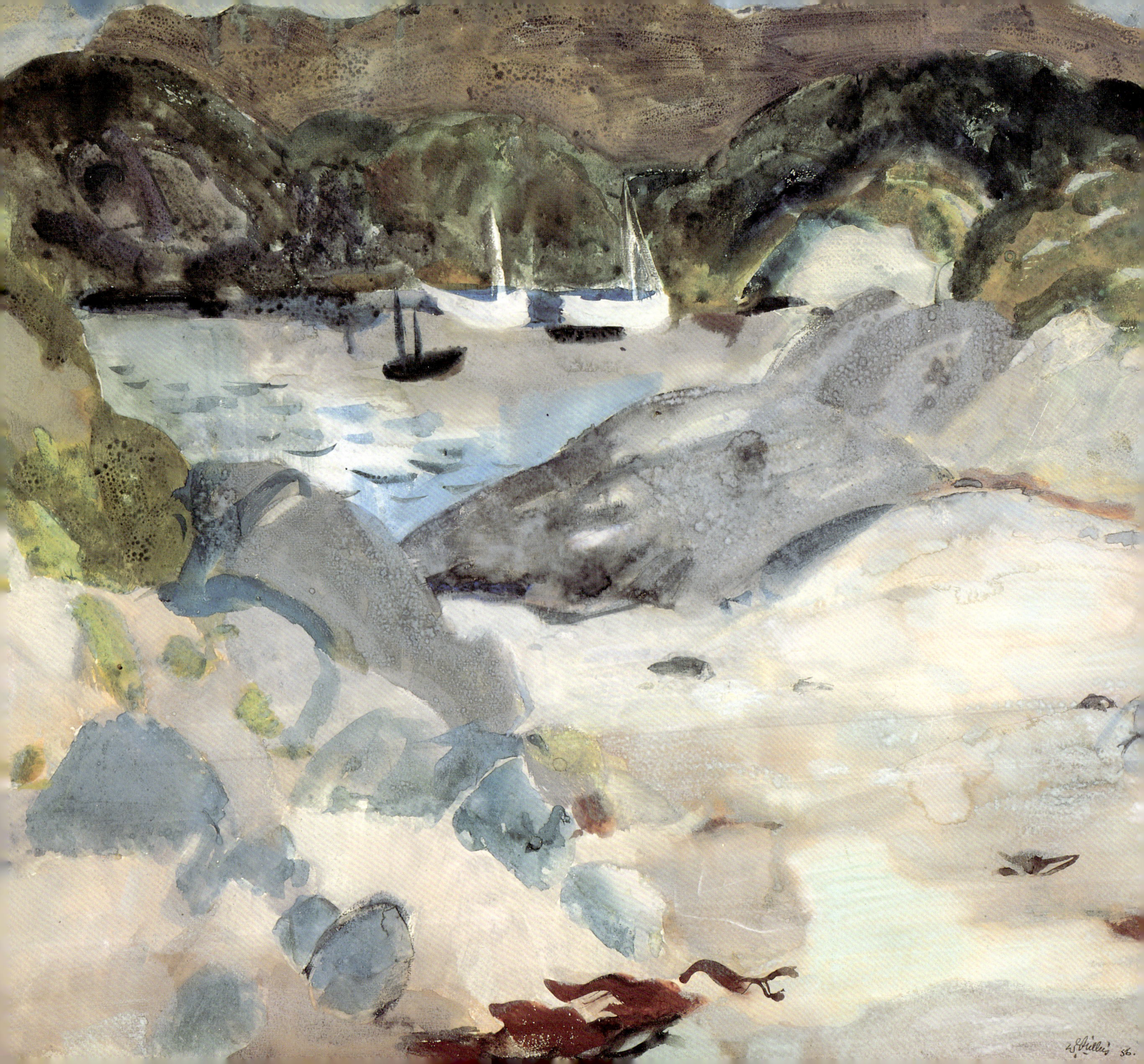

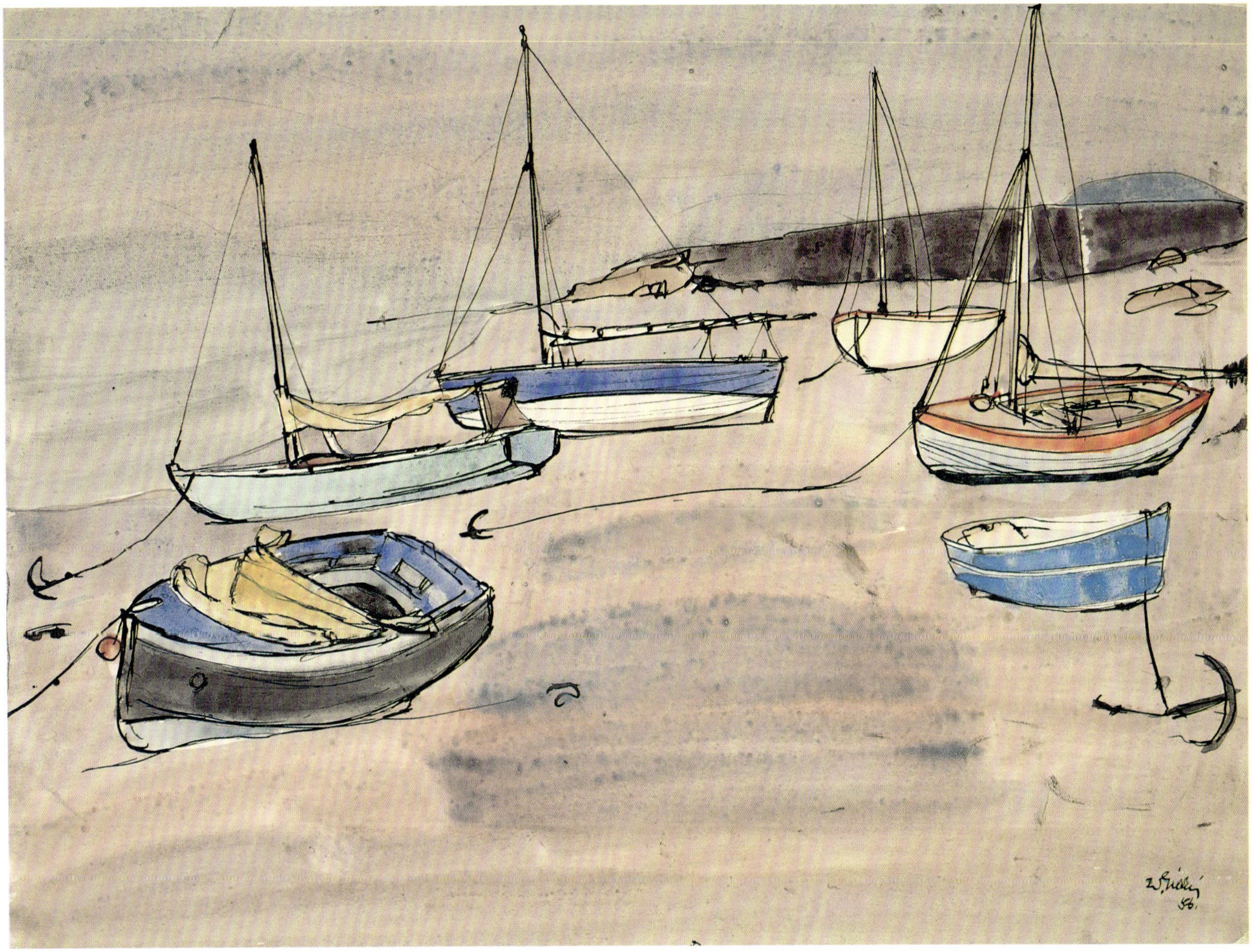

opposite

22 WHITE BOATS IN THE BAY
dated 1956 · catalogue 67

above

23 BEACHED BOATS, KIPPFORD
dated 1956 · catalogue 64

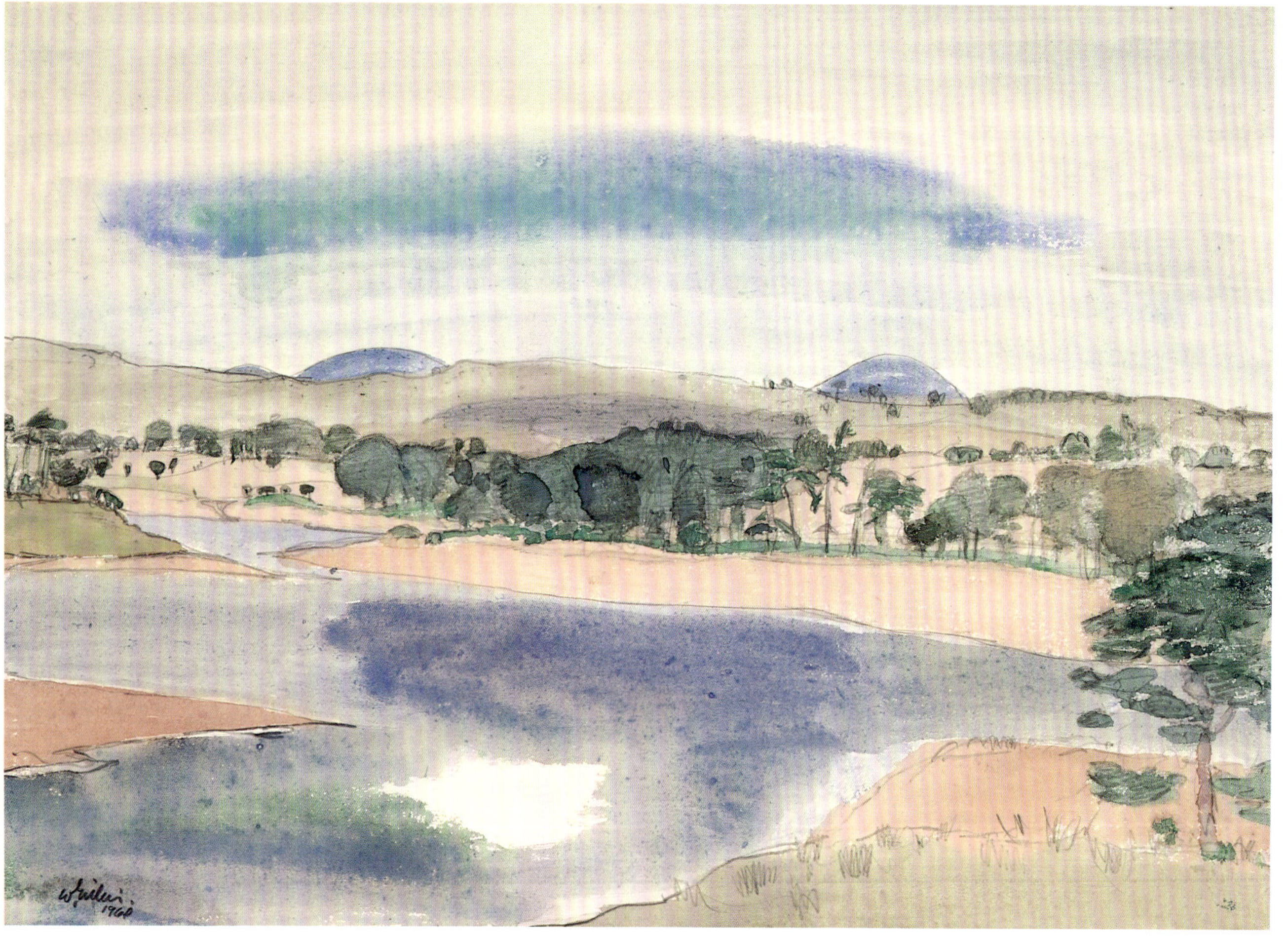

24 SUMMER, MOORFOOT
dated 1960 · catalogue 72

Catalogue

With the exception of catalogue 1, all works were bequeathed to the Scottish National Gallery of Modern Art by Dr R. A. Lillie in 1977.

All sizes are given in centimetres, height preceding width.

An asterix indicates that the work is illustrated in the colour plate section.

1*
WOODLAND PATH
dated 1926
watercolour and pencil on paper
28.2 × 36.1
bequeathed by Keith Andrews 1990

2
MORNING LIGHT, KIRCUDBRIGHT FARM
circa 1929
watercolour and pencil on paper
26.9 × 35.2

This and the following watercolour are likely to have been painted on the first painting trip Gillies made with John Maxwell in 1929 to the countryside around Maxwell's home town of Dalbeattie, in Kircudbrightshire.

3
NEAR KIRCUDBRIGHT
dated 1929
watercolour and pencil on paper
26.9 × 35

4*
MORAR
dated 1931
watercolour and gum arabic on paper
38.2 × 55.7

The west coast and in particular the area around Morar became one of Gillies's favourite destinations for painting expeditions in the 1930s.

We are down in Morar Bay, as usual but this year there are quite a lot of camps. However we are fairly high up and have a view both up to Morar River and down to the sea. Johny [John Maxwell] *is delighted with the place.*

Postcard from Gillies to his sister Emma, 1933 (Royal Scottish Academy Archive)

5*
SKYE HILLS FROM NEAR MORAR
circa 1931
watercolour and gouache on board
37.6 × 55.8

This is the view from our doorstep! Last nite it was really amazing with the Cuillins sailing on a raspberry jam sea like an immense blue and pink cake.

Postcard from John Maxwell to 'Miss Gillies' showing a view from the Scottish mainland to the Cuillins of Skye (Royal Scottish Academy Archive)

6*
A POOL
dated 1932
watercolour and black chalk on paper
27.8 × 38

7
MILTON
dated 1933
watercolour on paper
46.1 × 55.9

8*
THE STREET
circa 1933
watercolour and gouache on paper
50.5 × 63.1

9*
THE DARK POND
circa 1934
watercolour on paper
50.4 × 63.6

Gillies commented on this work:
I like this one because it is so different in theme and manner of using the medium. I did it on the spot … using a large hog's-hair brush which is a stiff one and, except for a few large, liquid washes, keeping the paint rather dry and bristly, only a broad effect was attempted, but with much thought given to its mood.

Still Life with Honesty: a film on Gillies's life and work produced for the Scottish Arts Council by OGAM Films 1969

10
HEAD OF THE GLEN
mid – late 1930s
watercolour and pencil on paper
55.5 × 73.5

11*
IN ARDNAMURCHAN
circa 1936
watercolour and gouache on paper
50.6 × 63

Gillies said about this work:
The mood of this one I like. There is a fine threat in the landscape. And I feel an honest, rather pathetic role is put into the drawing and seeing of the elderly people having the picnic among the rocks. My mother, sister and Aunt Margaret are the subjects.

Still Life with Honesty: a film on Gillies's life and work produced for the Scottish Arts Council by OGAM Films 1969

12
LOCH CARRON
circa 1936
watercolour on paper
50 × 63.2

Johny [John Maxwell] *and I are delighted with the district. D. M. Sutherland and family are at Plockton and we go down to see them at night – play Lexicon. We are just beginning to get some work done – watercolours so far. Very bad storm last night, rain and wind – tent collapsed middle of night but did not get wet. Fine again today.*

Postcard from Gillies to his sister Emma from Kyle, 27 August 1935 (Royal Scottish Academy Archive)

The area around Loch Carron and the Kyle of Lochalsh, which separates the Scottish mainland from Skye, provided inspiration for many of Gillies's watercolours (catalogue 32, 33, 35). David MacBeth Sutherland (1883–1973) taught at Edinburgh College of Art from 1918 until 1933 when he was appointed Head of Gray's School of Art, Aberdeen.

13
AUTUMN SO EARLY
circa 1937
watercolour on paper
25.3 × 35.4

14
SUILVEN, WESTER ROSS
dated 1937
watercolour and gouache on paper
50.7 × 64

15
RHYNIE
[verso: Study of a Tree]
Late 1930s – early 1940s
watercolour on paper [verso: black chalk]
56.2 × 76.7

16*
CROFTS, BONAR BRIDGE
circa 1938
watercolour and pen and ink on paper
66.5 × 79

Bonar Bridge and Spinningdale (catalogue 17) are situated on the Dornoch Firth in Easter Ross.

A lovely little place, plenty of sketching. I think we will be here for quite a while.

Postcard from Gillies to his sister Janet from Bonar Bridge (Royal Scottish Academy Archive)

17
SPINNINGDALE
circa 1938–39
watercolour, gouache and pen and ink on paper
50 × 63.2

18*
THE VILLAGE LETTER BOX
1940s
watercolour, gouache and pencil on paper
50.6 × 68.7

19
THE ROAD BETWEEN TEMPLE AND MIDDLETON
circa 1941
watercolour, gouache and pen and ink on paper
42 × 53.2

Gillies and his family moved to the Midlothian village of Temple in 1939.

I needed to live in the landscape I was painting and Temple, situated within a mile or two of the fine, bare, Moorfoot Hills and with the rich agricultural countryside of Midlothian within easy reach in the other direction, is just what I wanted. I had the whole Border countryside full of subject matter open to me.

Still Life with Honesty: a film on Gillies's life and work produced for the Scottish Arts Council by OGAM Films 1969

20*
WINTER AFTERNOON, TEMPLE
circa 1942
watercolour, gouache and pen and ink on paper
34.2 × 51.1

Gillies described the process of making this work:

I began with a very sketchy, loose pen line with much variation in strength and thickness, and then floated on mostly grey washes – many of them found around the edges of my paint box which I tend to leave uncleaned for this very purpose.

Still Life with Honesty: a film on Gillies's life and work produced for the Scottish Arts Council by OGAM Films 1969

21*
CASTLETON
circa 1944
watercolour and gouache on paper
37.2 × 44.7

22
TREES IN THE GLOAMING
dated 1944
watercolour and gouache on paper
46.3 × 55.6

23*
LANDSCAPE WITH HOUSES, TEMPLE
mid–1940s
watercolour and gouache on paper
50.6 × 63.7

24*
THE POND
circa 1945–48
watercolour, gouache and pen and ink on paper
68.5 × 53

25
DYKEHEAD, GLEN PROSEN
dated 1946
watercolour and pencil on paper
31.6 × 50.8

26
KIRRIEMUIR, THE ROODS
circa 1946
watercolour, pen and ink and pencil on paper
23.5 × 30.7

Gillies's mother was from Kirriemuir and Gillies and his family regularly spent holidays there.

27
MAIN STREET, KIRRIEMUIR
circa 1946
watercolour and pencil on paper
23.5 × 30.6

28
NORTH MUIR, KIRRIEMUIR
circa 1946
watercolour and pencil on paper
10.6 × 14.8

29
THE RED HOUSE, KIRRIEMUIR
dated 1946
watercolour and pen and ink on paper
23.6 × 30.7

30
THE TWO CHURCHES, KIRRIEMUIR
1946
watercolour, gum arabic and pencil on paper
47.9 × 61.7

31*
WIND ABOVE KIRRIEMUIR
dated 1946
watercolour and pen and ink on paper
23.9 × 31.2

32
BALMACARA
1947
watercolour and pencil on paper
24 × 27.1

33
BALMACARA
[verso: Balmacara]
circa 1947
watercolour and pencil on paper
[verso: pencil]
24.6 × 31.5

34
WINTER, CARRINGTON
dated 1947
watercolour, gouache and pencil on paper
20.4 × 25.9

35
THE RAINBOW, LETTERFEARN
circa 1947
watercolour on paper
51.6 × 63.5

36
THE GYLES, PITTENWEEM
circa 1947
watercolour and pen and ink on paper
47.9 × 62.2

From the late 1940s and through the 1950s Gillies made repeated visits to the fishing villages of Pittenweem, Anstruther (catalogue 39, 40, 41) and St Monance (catalogue 44, 45) on the east coast of Fife.

Arrived all safe. No accommodation so camping at Hew Lorimer's Kellie Castle, by Pittenweem. Food at Commercial Hotel Anstruther … Could you post li-lo … Sleeping bag is not soft enough.

Postcard from Gillies to his sister Janet from Anstruther, 1949 (Royal Scottish Academy Archive)

37
HAWKSNEST FARM
late 1940s
watercolour and pencil on paper
25.4 × 59

38
SNOW, TEMPLE
late 1940s
watercolour on paper
33.9 × 50.8

A view from Gillies's studio window.

39
ANSTRUTHER FROM THE HARBOUR WALL
1948
watercolour, gouache and pen and ink on paper
47.8 × 63.2

40
ANSTRUTHER HARBOUR
circa 1948
watercolour and pen and ink on paper
47.7 × 63.2

41
ANSTRUTHER
circa 1948
watercolour and pen and ink on paper
22.7 × 62.4

42*
THE FISHING BOAT
dated 1949
watercolour and pen and ink on paper
24.5 × 31.2

43
ROSEBERY RESERVOIR
circa 1949
watercolour and gum arabic on paper
38.3 × 57

44
ST MONANCE
circa 1949
watercolour and chalk on paper
24.7 × 31.5

45*
ST MONANCE FROM THE HARBOUR
circa 1949
watercolour and pen and ink on paper (two sheets joined)
24.6 × 39.9

46*
WINTER, TEMPLE (BACK OF HOUSES)
circa 1949
watercolour and pen and ink on paper
50.2 × 67.1

47
GARDENSTOWN OLD CEMETERY
dated 1950
watercolour and pencil on paper
24.7 × 31.7

48*
GARDENSTOWN – RED CLIFF
circa 1950
watercolour and pencil on paper
24.7 × 31.6

49
VALLEY PAST HERIOT
dated 1950
watercolour, gouache and pen and ink on paper
36 × 55.4

50
WOODED LANDSCAPE, LOTHIAN
dated 1950
watercolour and pen and ink on paper
47.9 × 63

51
THE PENTLANDS, WINTER
circa 1950–52
watercolour and pencil on paper
25.5 × 35.5

52
HAY TIME, TEMPLE
Early 1950s
watercolour and gouache on paper
55 × 67.2

53
EARLY EVENING
1950s
watercolour and pencil on paper
39.3 × 57.1

54*
NEAR HOWGATE
dated 1951
watercolour and pencil on paper
25.2 × 35.4

55
FARM ON THE MELDONS ROAD
dated 1951
watercolour and pencil on paper
37.5 × 55.6

56*
MARCH, MOORFOOT
dated 1951
watercolour and pencil on paper
66.3 × 55

57
MORAY HARBOUR
dated 1951
watercolour, gouache and ink on paper
48.2 × 61.5

58
PENNAN
circa 1951
watercolour, gouache and pen and ink on paper
25.2 × 35.2

59
NEAR ROMANNO BRIDGE
circa 1951
watercolour and pencil on paper
25.3 × 35.4

60
WINTER
dated 1951
watercolour and pencil
25.5 × 35.5

61
BORDER VALLEY (WITH TRAIN)
circa 1953
charcoal and ink wash on paper
35.4 × 42.4

62
KENMORE
mid – late 1950s
watercolour and black chalk on paper
24.5 × 31.7

63
EYEMOUTH (BOATS WITH NETS)
circa 1955–56
watercolour and pencil on paper
23.4 × 35.6

64*
BEACHED BOATS, KIPPFORD
dated 1956
watercolour, pen and ink and pencil on paper
27.8 × 38

65
ST ABBS, NETS
circa 1956
watercolour and pencil on paper
25.4 × 35.5

66
BELOW STOW
dated 1956
watercolour and pencil on paper
24 × 27.4

67*
WHITE BOATS IN THE BAY
dated 1956
watercolour and gouache on paper
50.1 × 67.3

68
BELOW HERIOT, OTHER SIDE OF THE RIVER
dated 1956
watercolour and pencil on paper
24.7 × 31.5

69
THE ROADMAN'S HOUSE, LYNE
dated 1957
watercolour and black chalk on paper
25.6 × 35.3

70
UPLAND HARVEST
dated 1957
watercolour and pencil on paper
25.4 × 35.4

71
DREVA
dated 1959
watercolour, gouache and pencil on paper
34 × 51.2

72*
SUMMER, MOORFOOT
dated 1960
watercolour and pencil on paper
25.2 × 35.5

Referring to this work, Gillies said: *This was done … during a dry summer. I was struck by the happy harmony between the water and the pinks of the banks and the various difference in the blues of the sky and of the water. It was a slight subject and I treated it as simply as I knew how.*

Still Life with Honesty: a film on Gillies's life and work produced for the Scottish Arts Council by OGAM Films 1969

73
ROAD TO THE FARM
dated 1960
watercolour and pencil on paper
25.4 × 35.4

74
THE LOCH, PORTMORE
1960s
watercolour and pencil on paper
24 × 27.2

75
FROM THE GARDEN, TEMPLE
dated 1963
watercolour and black chalk on paper
25.5 × 35.4

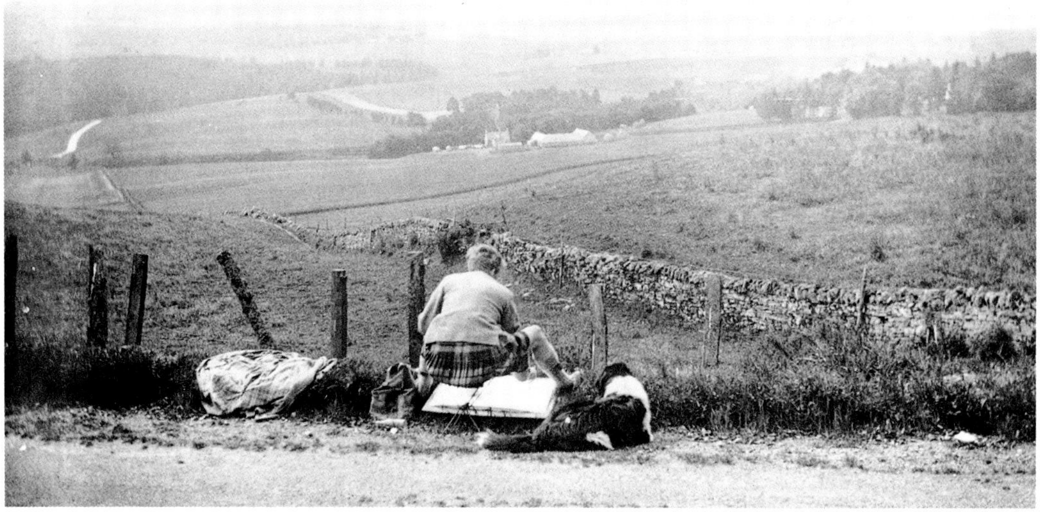

The artist at work

Chronology

1898
Born 21 September, Haddington, East Lothian, son of John (born 1856) and Emma Gillies (née Smith, born 1864) and brother of Janet (born 1896) and Emma (born 1900).
Educated at the Knox Institute, Haddington.

1916
Enrolled at Edinburgh College of Art.

1917
Called up for National Service.
Drafted with the Scottish Rifles to France where he saw service around Arras. Wounded and gassed and returned to Scotland in 1918.

1919
Resumed studies at Edinburgh College of Art.

1921
Death of Gillies's father.
Awarded Minor Travelling Bursary.

1922
Awarded Diploma in Drawing and Painting and post-Diploma Scholarship providing studio facilities for a further year's study.
Became a founder member of the exhibiting society the 1922 Group. The Group's exhibitions were held in Edinburgh from 1923–29.

1923
Awarded Travelling Scholarship and, with fellow recipient William Geissler, went to Paris to study under André Lhote, and then travelled to Italy.

1924
Returned to Scotland.
Appointed Assistant Art Master at the Royal Academy, Inverness.

1925
Appointed part-time lecturer in School of Drawing and Painting, Edinburgh College of Art.

1928
Gillies's family moved from Haddington to 162 Willowbrae Road, Edinburgh.
Joint exhibition with Frances Hodgkins, St George's Gallery, London.
Work first exhibited at the Royal Scottish Academy.

1932
Invited to become member of the exhibiting society, the Society of Eight. The Society's exhibitions were held in Edinburgh from 1912–1938.

1934
Appointed full-time lecturer, Edinburgh College of Art.
Work first exhibited at the Society of Scottish Artists.

1935
Death of Gillies's sister, Emma.

1937
Elected professional member of the Society of Scottish Artists.

1939
Gillies's family moved to Temple, Midlothian.

1940
Elected Associate of the Royal Scottish Academy.

1942
Work included in the exhibition *Six Scottish Painters*, Reid and Lefevre, London.

1946
Appointed Head of the School of Drawing and Painting, Edinburgh College of Art.

1947
Elected Royal Scottish Academician.

1948
Solo exhibition at the French Institute, Edinburgh (drawn from the collection of Dr R. A. Lillie).

1949
Solo exhibition at The Scottish Gallery, Edinburgh. (The first of Gillies's many exhibitions held at The Scottish Gallery).

1950
Elected member of the Royal Scottish Society of Painters in Watercolour.

1951
Work included in the exhibition *60 Paintings for '51*, Festival of Britain, South Bank, London.

1953
Solo exhibition, *The Scottish Scene*, The National Trust for Scotland, Edinburgh (drawn from the collection of Dr R. A. Lillie).

1954
Arts Council exhibition, *Paintings, watercolours and drawings by W. G. Gillies and John Maxwell*, New Burlington Galleries, London.

1957
Awarded CBE.

1960
Appointed Principal of Edinburgh College of Art.
Death of Gillies's sister, Janet.

1962
Work included in the exhibition *Modern Scottish Paintings from the Collection of Dr Lillie*, Scottish National Gallery of Modern Art, Edinburgh.

1963
Elected President of the Royal Scottish Society of Painters in Watercolour.
Death of Gillies's mother.

1964
Elected Associate of the Royal Academy.

1966
Received Honorary Degree of Doctor of Letters from Edinburgh University.
Elected Fellow of the Educational Institute of Scotland.
Retired as Principal of Edinburgh College of Art.

1969
Retired as President of the Royal Scottish Society of Painters in Watercolour.

1970
Knighted in recognition of his services to art in Scotland.
Retrospective exhibition, *W. G. Gillies*, Royal Scottish Academy and Scottish Arts Council Gallery, Edinburgh.

1971
Elected Royal Academician.

1973
Died 15 April, Temple.

SELECT BIBLIOGRAPHY

Mungo Campbell, *The Line of Tradition*, National Galleries of Scotland, Edinburgh, 1993

Thomas Elder Dickson, 'W. G. Gillies' in *The Studio*, London, Vol.v, no.166, 1960, pp.14–18

Thomas Elder Dickson, *W. G. Gillies*, Edinburgh University Press, 1974

Ian Finlay, *Art in Scotland*, Oxford University Press, 1948

Jack Firth, *Scottish Watercolour Painting*, The Ramsay Head Press, Edinburgh, 1979

W. G. Gillies, catalogue, with introduction by Thomas Elder Dickson, to retrospective exhibition organised by the Scottish Arts Council, Edinburgh, 1970

William Gillies & The Scottish Landscape, catalogue, with text by Margaret Mackay and Victoria Keller, to Scottish Arts Council touring exhibition, Edinburgh, 1980

Julian Halsby, *Scottish Watercolours 1740–1940*, B. T. Batsford Ltd, London, 1986

Keith Hartley *et al.*, *Scottish Art since 1900*, National Galleries of Scotland / Lund Humphries, London, 1989

Duncan Macmillan, *Scottish Art 1460–1990*, Mainstream, Edinburgh, 1990

The Scottish Scene, catalogue, with essay by George Scott-Moncrieff, to exhibition of watercolours and drawings by Gillies (from the collection of Dr R. A. Lillie), The National Trust for Scotland, Edinburgh, 1953

Alistair Smart, 'Art of W. G. Gillies' in *The Scottish Art Review*, Vol.v, no.2, pp.11–15

W. Gordon Smith, *W. G. Gillies, A Very Still Life*, Atelier Books, Edinburgh, 1991

Anne Wishart ed., *The Society of Scottish Artists, The First 100 Years*, Society of Scottish Artists, Edinburgh, 1991

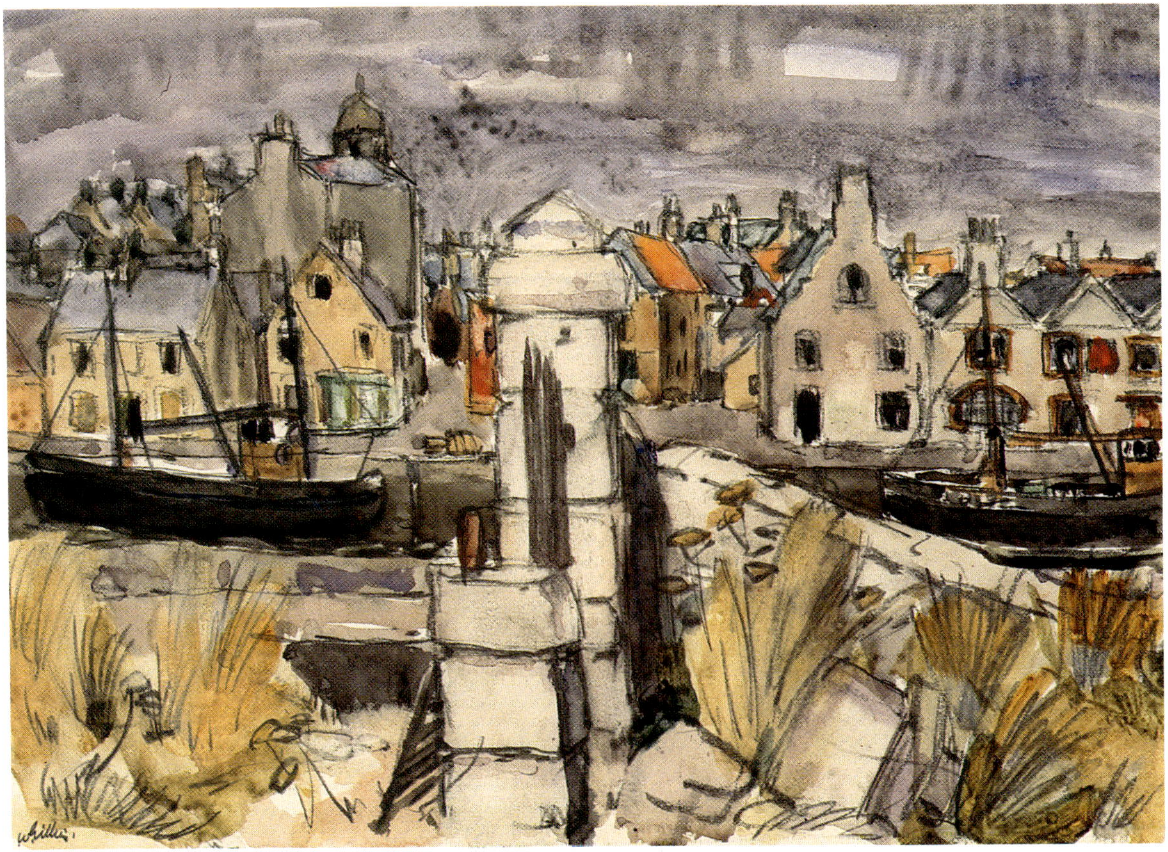

Eyemouth 24